Before the building of canals, water t... was restricted to a few natural ancie... ...ors that had been improved so that barges could collect goods from ships at coastal ports and deliver to inland port locations. The only other commercial transport available was by horse and cart over rough track roads. The building of canals in the 18th and 19th centuries revolutionised a whole new commercial transportation system and this new system rapidly grew to a network of over 5,000 miles of inland waterways. This system greatly helped the Industrial Revolution carrying British products from inland areas sometimes hundreds of miles to the sea. This lasted until the coming of the railways after which use of canals declined and by the start of WW2 over half the mileage was derelict. Rivers fared better helped by the development of river leisure boating.

In 1946 the Inland Waterways Association (IWA) was founded and forward thinking enthusiasts campaigned to rescue our canal heritage. Thanks to their endeavours now over 60 years on, there are over 3,000 miles of navigable canals and rivers open for us all to enjoy to use for leisure and relaxation be it for boating, walking or fishing. Each year many thousands of people enjoy the delights of inland waterway boating either in a narrowboat or cruiser. Some start with a holiday on a hire boat and go on to purchase their own boat and some are choosing to throw off the shackles of life on land and live permanently on their boat. No wonder, it is something that can be enjoyed by all ages and you meet delightful, helpful and interesting people on the way.

As with everything to get the most enjoyment out of an activity you need to know what you are doing. With this book and by taking the RYA Training Course it accompanies, you will be able to confidently make the most of your inland waterways adventures. I have distilled over 40 years of inland waterways into these pages to help make your cruises safe, enjoyable and above all else fun.

Windlass to the ready...
Andrew Newman

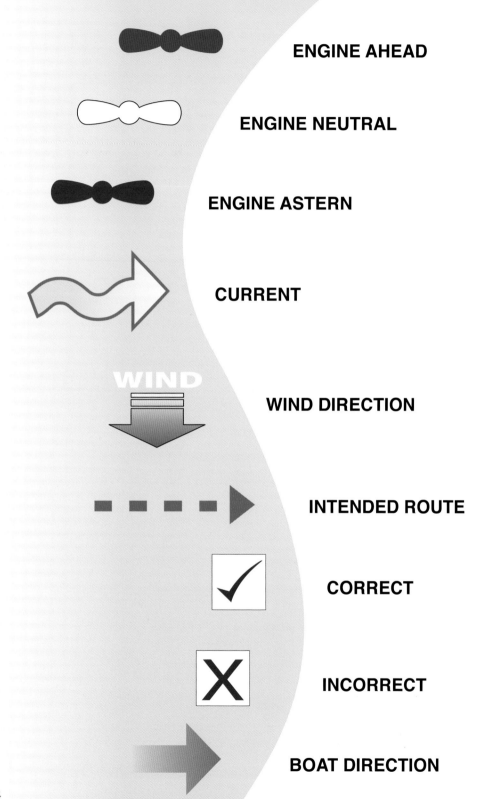

ENGINE AHEAD

ENGINE NEUTRAL

ENGINE ASTERN

CURRENT

WIND DIRECTION

INTENDED ROUTE

CORRECT

INCORRECT

BOAT DIRECTION

Inland waterways handbook

by Andrew Newman

Second edition 2010
Reprinted April 2011
Updated May 2013
Updated March 2014
Updated January 2015
Reprinted March 2016
Reprinted January 2017
Reprinted June 2017
Reprinted September 2017
Reprinted November 2018
Reprinted January 2020

Technical Editor: Andrew Norton

We recommend that you carry the relevant navigation handbook on board for the areas you intend to cruise.

Published by
**The Royal Yachting Association
RYA House, Ensign Way,
Hamble, Southampton SO31 4YA
Tel: 02380 604 100
Web: www.rya.org.uk
Follow us on Twitter @RYAPublications or on YouTube
We welcome feedback on our publications at
publications@rya.org.uk
You can check content updates for
RYA publications at
www.rya.org.uk/go/bookschangelog
ISBN: 978-1906-435-349
RYA Order Code G102**

British Cataloguing in Publication Data:
A catalogue record of this book is available
from the British Library.

*Cover Design and Illustrations:
Pete Galvin.
Layout: Creativebyte.
Photos courtesy of
Blakes Holiday Boating, Broom, Gary Blake,
Paul Bullock, Pete Galvin, and the RYA.
The RYA acknowledges the contribution
made to this course by the author
Andrew Newman.
Printed in China through World Print Ltd.*

The RYA would like to thank the following organisations for their assistance with this new edition and their support in endorsing it to their members and the public.

Association of Waterways Cruising Clubs (AWCC)

The Yacht Basin, Camley Street
London NW1 0PL
Email: info@awcc.org.uk
Website: www.awcc.org.uk

AWCC exists to secure the interests of its member clubs and their members in all matters relating to their enjoyment of the navigable waterways of the United Kingdom.

The Barge Association (DBA)

Cormorant, Spade Oak Reach, Cookham
Maidenhead SL6 9RQ
Tel: 07000 227437
Email: info@barges.org
Website: www.barges.org

The DBA aims to bring together people interested in barges and barging, both in the UK and Europe.

British Marine Federation (BMF)

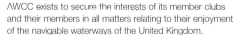

Marine House, Thorpe Lea Road,
Egham, Surrey TW20 8BF
Tel: 01784 223600
Email: info@britishmarine.co.uk
Website: www.britishmarine.co.uk

The British Marine Federation is the trade association for businesses operating in the UK marine industry. With more than 1500 member companies, it represents over 75 per cent of the industry's turnover. The British Marine Federation is recognised by the government as the voice of the UK boating industry.

Canal & River Trust

Head Office, First Floor North
Station House, 500 Elder Gate
Milton Keynes MK9 1BB
Tel: 0303 040 4040
Email: customer.services@canalrivertrust.org.uk
Website: www.canalrivertrust.org.uk

In an increasingly fast-paced and crowded world, the Canal & River Trust's historic canals and rivers provide a local haven for people and nature. They're the charity entrusted with the care of 2,000 miles of waterways in England and Wales.

Broads Authority

Dragonfly House
2 Gilders Way, Norwich NR3 1UB
Tel: 01603 610734 Fax: 01603 765710
Email: broads@broads-authority.gov.uk
Website: broads-authority.gov.uk

The Broads Authority has the status of a national park authority and manages the 125 miles of inland rivers and 40 broads (shallow lakes) for conservation, navigation and recreation.

The Environment Agency

Rio House, Waterside Drive,
Aztec West, Almondsbury,
Bristol BS32 4UD
Tel: 01454 624411 Fax: 01454 624014
Email: enquiries@environment-agency.gov.uk
Website: www.environment-agency.gov.uk

The Environment Agency's aim is to manage the healthy growth of waterways for leisure, business, local communities and wildlife.

National Association of Boat Owners (NABO)

Freepost (BM8367),
Birmingham, B31 2BR
Email: gen.sec@nabo.org.uk
Website: www.nabo.org.uk

NABO is an association body that represents boat owners on inland and estuarial waters.

Contents

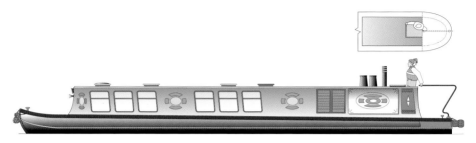

TRADITIONAL NARROWBOAT
Suitable for most narrow and broad canals and rivers.
Up to 21.3m (70 feet) long (maximum length for most canals).

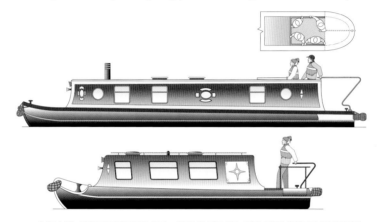

CANAL NARROWBOAT - SEMI TRAD OR CRUISER STERN
Usually have a larger rear deck, ideal for the family.
Both types have steel hulls and are suitable for use on narrow canals.

BROAD BEAM and DUTCH BARGES
Large craft, comfortable as a live-aboard vessel often used in mainland Europe.

WIDE BEAM INLAND CRUISER
(CENTRE COCKPIT)
Popular on the Norfolk Broads, Thames and other larger waterways.
The wind can affect steering control on both designs.

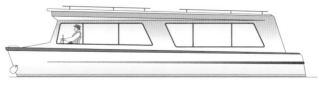

FORWARD STEERING CRUISER
The stern is harder to control and see when manoeuvring. Wind can effect steering control.

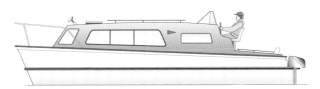

SMALL NARROW BEAM OUTBOARD CRUISER

Very popular on canals and smaller rivers. Economical to buy and run. Easy to steer and trailerable. The vulnerable outboard motor can be a disadvantage.

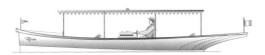

ELECTRIC LAUNCH

Electric power is growing in popularity for inland craft, as it is silent, and causes no pollution to the local environment, or annoyance to other users of the waterway.

SEA / ESTUARY OUTBOARD CRUISER

Good beginner's boat. Inexpensive to buy and trailerable. Ideal for weekends away spent exploring isolated waterways.

SEA / ESTUARY CRUISER

Popular on wide rivers. Well equipped, comfortable and powerful, but expensive to buy and run. Capable of sea passages. Limited inland use due to height and width restrictions.

CRUISER

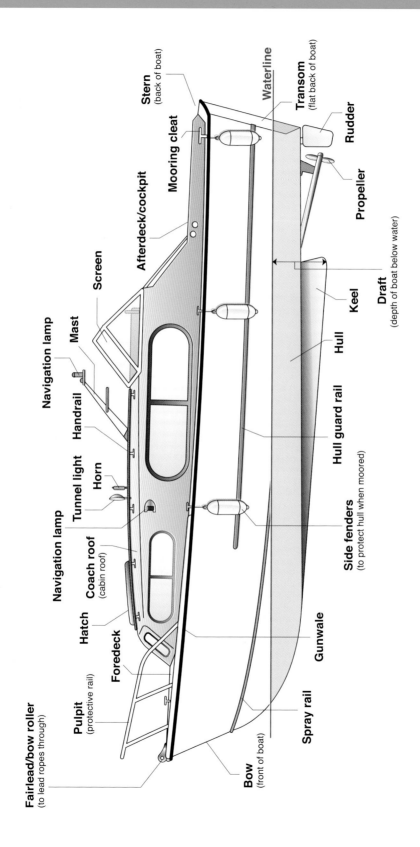

Stern
(back of boat)

Waterline

Transom
(flat back of boat)

Rudder

Mooring cleat

Propeller

Afterdeck/cockpit

Draft
(depth of boat below water)

Keel

Screen

Hull

Mast

Navigation lamp

Handrail

Hull guard rail

Tunnel light

Horn

Navigation lamp

Side fenders
(to protect hull when moored)

Coach roof
(cabin roof)

Hatch

Gunwale

Foredeck

Pulpit
(protective rail)

Spray rail

Fairlead/bow roller
(to lead ropes through)

Bow
(front of boat)

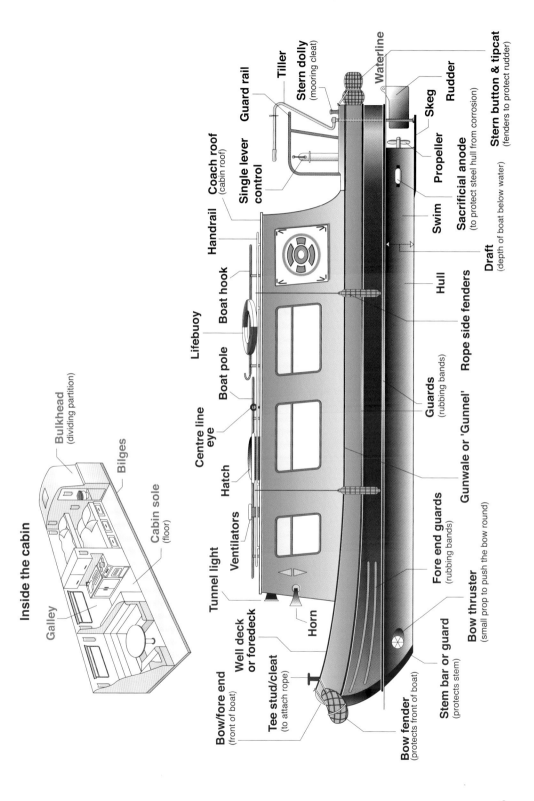

Inside the cabin

Galley

Bulkhead
(dividing partition)

Bilges

Cabin sole
(floor)

Tunnel light

Ventilators

Hatch

Centre line
eye

Boat pole

Lifebuoy

Boat hook

Handrail

Coach roof
(cabin roof)

Single lever
control

Guard rail

Tiller

Stern dolly
(mooring cleat)

Waterline

Rudder

Skeg

Propeller

Sacrificial anode
(to protect steel hull from corrosion)

Stern button & tipcat
(fenders to protect rudder)

Swim

Draft
(depth of boat below water)

Hull

Rope side fenders

Guards
(rubbing bands)

Gunwale or 'Gunnel'

Fore end guards
(rubbing bands)

Bow thruster
(small prop to push the bow round)

Horn

Bow/fore end
(front of boat)

Well deck
or foredeck

Tee stud/cleat
(to attach rope)

Stem bar or guard
(protects stem)

Bow fender
(protects front of boat)

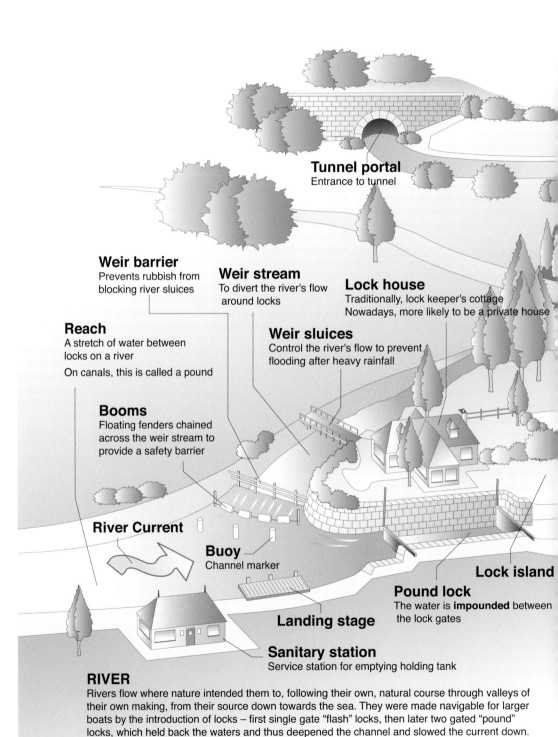

Tunnel portal
Entrance to tunnel

Weir barrier
Prevents rubbish from
blocking river sluices

Weir stream
To divert the river's flow
around locks

Lock house
Traditionally, lock keeper's cottage
Nowadays, more likely to be a private house

Reach
A stretch of water between
locks on a river

On canals, this is called a pound

Weir sluices
Control the river's flow to prevent
flooding after heavy rainfall

Booms
Floating fenders chained
across the weir stream to
provide a safety barrier

River Current

Buoy
Channel marker

Lock island

Pound lock
The water is **impounded** between
the lock gates

Landing stage

Sanitary station
Service station for emptying holding tank

RIVER
Rivers flow where nature intended them to, following their own, natural course through valleys of
their own making, from their source down towards the sea. They were made navigable for larger
boats by the introduction of locks – first single gate "flash" locks, then later two gated "pound"
locks, which held back the waters and thus deepened the channel and slowed the current down.

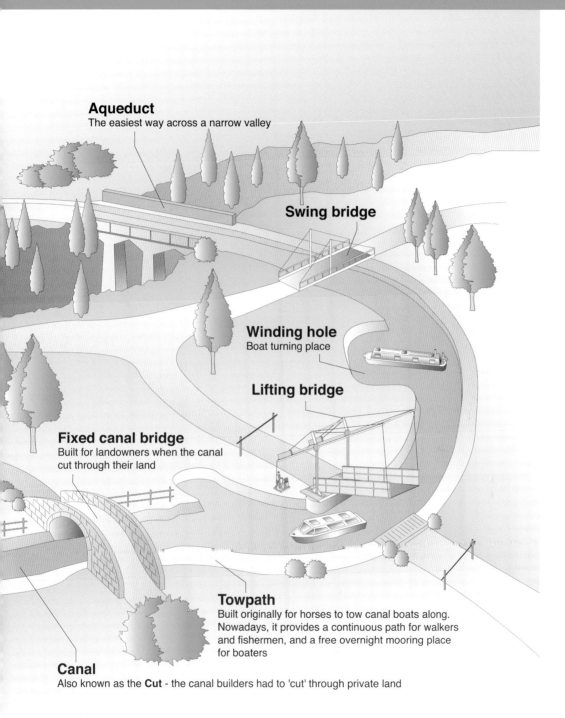

Aqueduct
The easiest way across a narrow valley

Swing bridge

Winding hole
Boat turning place

Lifting bridge

Fixed canal bridge
Built for landowners when the canal
cut through their land

Towpath
Built originally for horses to tow canal boats along.
Nowadays, it provides a continuous path for walkers
and fishermen, and a free overnight mooring place
for boaters

Canal
Also known as the **Cut** - the canal builders had to 'cut' through private land

CANAL
Canals were built to take boats where no river could go - across valleys, and over or
through hills. Locks 'lift' boats up or down hill.

Before you set off

- Check that your boat has a current Navigation Authority licence for the waters which you intend to cruise.

- Check that your boat is in good condition and has a current Boat Safety Scheme certificate. This certificate is like a "Boat MOT" and is renewable every four years. All UK navigation authorities require one in order for you to obtain a boat licence. If your boat is new then it will have a "Declaration of Conformity" certificate to the "Recreational Craft Directive" or RCD and there will be an Identification Plate attached on board showing the vessel's i.d. number and maximum crew capacity. This takes the place of the Boat Safety Certificate until the craft is four years old.

- Make sure that your boat is insured at least for third party risks. All navigation authorities require this.

- Ensure that you and your crew know how to handle the boat and the conditions you may encounter on your cruise.

- Obtain the free navigational information guides from the Authorities whose waters you are going to cruise. These detail the rules & regulations as well as a mass of navigation, safety and mooring information. On rivers such as the Thames, Severn and Trent they also include lock opening hours and details of strong stream warnings, bridge clearances and tidal conditions.

- Make sure that you carry maps or guide books covering the waterways you are cruising. These are essential reading on passage as they show in great detail all the bridges (with numbers on canals), mileages, moorings and locks. They also list where all the facilities are, including water and refuse points, toilet disposal facilities, boatyards and fuelling points as well as where the shops…and pubs…are located!

- Plan your cruise. Allow plenty of time so you can always arrive in daylight. It is not advisable to cruise after dark or in bad visibility. When working out your schedule, take into account the speed restrictions.

- Check that your water and fuel tanks are full.

Lifejackets/Buoyancy Aids

There is quite a difference between the various types of buoyancy aids and lifejackets. In general terms:

- A buoyancy aid is designed to keep a conscious person afloat.

- An automatically inflating lifejacket is designed to support an unconscious person afloat, with their nose and mouth clear of the water.

Children's lifejackets (100N) and buoyancy aids should be fitted with crutch straps, so the jacket stays on if the child has to be lifted out of the water, and D-rings to allow harness lines to be attached.

It is sensible to wear a lifejacket, especially near locks, deep or fast flowing water and at night. We recommend that children, non-swimmers and those with disabilities wear a lifejacket or buoyancy aid at all times.

Children

Ensure that children are supervised at all times on or off the boat. This is especially important around locks.

NEVER jump across from boat to bank or bank to boat. Bring the boat in close, if you cannot try another mooring!

Equipment checklist

Make sure that you and the crew know where to find and use the following:

- Lifebelt. Lifeline (if supplied).
- Lifejackets.
- Anchor. For rivers, the rope and chain should be a combined length of at least six times the deepest part of the river.
- Fire extinguishers and fire blanket.
- Emergency shut-offs for battery, gas and fuel.

- Bilge pump.
- Emergency torch.
- Mooring ropes – long enough to stretch from your boat to the bollard and back in a deep lock.
- Mooring stakes and hammer.
- Horn.
- First aid kit.
- Boat pole and/or hook.
- Two windlasses (handles for operating locks.)

What to wear

- Loose, casual clothing.
- Non-slip shoes are most suitable for wet slippery lock areas and muddy towpaths. (Some deck shoes have poor grip on wet grass). Wellingtons should not be worn.

- Waterproof clothing is advisable as most canal boats have outside steering positions, and tunnels drip.
- As with any outdoor pursuits, sunhats, sunglasses, and suitable sun block are highly recommended.

Inland cruising is an extremely safe pastime but the following precautions should be taken:

Be aware
- Make sure that your crew know the importance of keeping their head, arms and legs inboard when near locks, bridges and tunnels. Keep within the profile of the boat.
- Sitting on the roof is a great way to see the countryside but be aware of overhanging tree branches which may harbour fishing tackle, hooks etc! Be prepared to lay flat or even get down in a hurry!
- The helmsman should warn the crew when he sees a potential hazard ahead such as a low bridge, or if the boat is about to bump into something.
- If you have passengers sitting in the front well or on the front deck make sure they are not dangling their legs or arms over the side.

Use the grab rail
- When boarding or stepping off the boat remember the old Navy expression "One hand for the ship and one hand for you". Hang on tight to the grab / handrails when walking on the side decks and watch where you put your feet! The helmsman should be prepared to stop the propeller should someone slip!
- Keep boat poles away from the grab rail so you do not grab the pole by mistake.
- Walk through the boat and not outside whenever possible.

Don't overload
- Don't allow too many people on the roof at once as the boat could become top heavy and roll over! Restrict the numbers to 50% of the number of berths.
- NEVER carry more people aboard than the maximum number stated on the RCD plate or in the boat's handbook or safety information folder. The legal maximum on any pleasure boat, however large, is 12.

Walk - don't run
- Surfaces can be wet and slippery – especially around locks.

Use fenders

- Never fend off using your arms or legs. The speed and weight of the boat may be greater than you realise and can cause serious injury.
- When coming in to moor, have a fender (on a line) ready to cushion the impact.
- Use larger fenders to keep the boat off awkward obstructions - be aware of vulnerable windows and cabin sides.

Don't swim

- Unfortunately, waterways are often used for illegal dumping. Submerged old bicycles and supermarket trolleys etc, are potential hazards.
- There may be dangerous currents, especially near weirs and locks.
- The water can be very cold, even in summer.
- Water quality may be poor. Do not drink or let your pets drink the water.
- If you or one of your crew falls in the water be aware of Weil's Disease. See Man Overboard on page 35.

Don't drink and drive

- As relevant to boats as it is to cars.

Moor up before nightfall

- It can be dangerous to go boating at night.
- Boating after dark is not permitted by hire boat companies.

Bottled gas, used for cookers, fridges and heaters, is perfectly safe if handled correctly but it can be dangerous if fumes escape.

If you smell gas

1 Get everyone outside.

2 Turn the gas off at source.

3 Ventilate the area.

4 On cruisers with removable floors, use a bucket or bowl to bail the gas over the side. On narrowboats, if you are able to access a pump-out station, open the cabin bilge hatch and pump out the trapped gas. Use a small hand operated manual pump and a hose to pump it over the side.

5 **Do not** use any electrical switches including bilge pumps, lights, etc, until you are sure that the gas has dispersed.

Gas is heavier than air and if there is a leak, it will accumulate in the bilges. It only takes a small spark to ignite.

Sensible precautions

• Switch off all gas appliances when not in use.

• Turn off the bottle(s) overnight or when you leave the boat, even if only for a day or two. However, if you are using the boat and have gas central heating or a gas fridge this will not be possible. In this case, be extra vigilant and aware of which appliances are running and check their operation frequently.

• Turn off all gas appliances before you change the gas bottle.

• Store gas bottles in outside lockers which self-drain overboard.

• Do not keep spare gas bottles inside the boat.

• Fit a gas detector and test it regularly.

• Keep ventilators open and clear of obstructions.

• Do not use or store stoves with a portable gas bottle inside the cabin.

ELECTRICITY/SHORE POWER

- Always attach the connection to the boat before plugging into the shore supply.
- Check your circuit breaker regularly.
- Ensure the lead is not a trip hazard.
- If charging batteries, ensure good ventilation.
- Ensure the lead cannot become trapped and chafed between boat hull and bank.

VENTILATION

Make sure that exhaust fumes cannot build up inside the boat.

All cooking and heating appliances can produce carbon monoxide if not properly ventilated.

Carbon monoxide poisoning can be a killer. The first signs are headaches, tiredness, sickness and dizziness. It is strongly recommended that you fit a Carbon Monoxide Detector.

Ensure adequate ventilation throughout the cabin.

BOAT SAFETY SCHEME

Boat Safety

The Canal & River Trust and the Environment Agency introduced the Boat Safety Scheme to set boat construction standards and the safe installation of gas and fuel systems, fire extinguishers and much more besides.

All boat owners should comply. **The Boat Safety Scheme has now been adopted by all navigation authorities.**
Visit boatsafetyscheme.org for more details.

PETROL

- Petrol vapour is explosive.
- Always switch your engine off before refuelling.
- Also turn off all naked lights, such as water heater pilot lights.
- Do not smoke or cook when refuelling.
- Never fill your tank in a lock.
- Do not allow fumes from refuelling to fill the boat – put boat covers up first.
- If there has been a leak, do not start the engine until the spillage has been cleared up.
- If there is petrol or fumes inside the boat, do not start the engine or relight pilot lights until the bilges are clear.
- Fill portable outboard petrol tanks away from the boat.
- Ensure that hose connections are sound and leak free.
- Most inboard petrol boats have blowers which should be run for a few minutes before starting the engine.

DIESEL

Many inland craft have diesel engines which are more economical and less hazardous than petrol.

- Take care not to spill when refuelling.
- Keep the tank vents clear.
- Do not fill with fuel at the same time as you are filling with water.

PRECAUTIONS

- Make sure that the crew know where fire extinguishers and fire blankets are kept, and how to use them.
- Plan your escape route and keep it clear.
- Fit a smoke alarm.
- Do not use a BBQ on the boat.

If you have a fire onboard

- First, get the boat to a bank.
- Evacuate the crew to a safe location.
- Call the Fire Services if necessary.

Use of a fire extinguisher

- Keep the extinguisher upright.
- Aim at the base of the fire.
- If the fire is in the engine compartment, only open the lid as far as you have to.
- Do not breathe the smoke - burning plastic is poisonous.

If someone's clothing is alight

- Quickly knock the casualty over onto the floor so that the flames rise away from their face.
- Smother the flames with a fire blanket or wet jacket/blanket. Wrap this around them and roll them over to extinguish the flames.

Do not use water on fires involving oil, diesel, petrol or electrics.

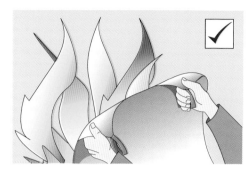

Fire blankets are useful for small galley fires. Hold like this to protect your hands.

Solid Fuel Stoves

- Ensure that stoves are firmly mounted on a heatproof solid base with fireproof material protecting bulkheads and cabin sides.
- Ideally store fuel in purpose made storage areas. It is not recommended that solid fuel be stored on the roof.
- Regular sweeping of the external chimney and flue will prevent build up of soot.
- Never run the stove with the stove door open.
- Do not put anything on the stove unless it is designed for that purpose.

WASTE DISPOSAL

It is illegal to discharge toilets into the waterway and there are plenty of pump-out stations at locks, boatyards and marinas (details from relevant navigation authorities).

Pump out station.

On Canal & River Trust (C&RT) navigations you will need a Watermate Key to access the pump out facilities. Only certain C&RT sanitary stations allow for manual self pump-out operation. See the instructions at each site for guidance on this. The Canal & River Trust and the Environment Agency have introduced self pump-out machines at many locations which need a payment card to operate them. These are available from lock keepers and C&RT marinas and offices. When you use one be aware that you only get a short time in which to complete the process (around seven minutes), once you put the card in, so make sure you get everything ready before you start the machine!

With a holding tank, make sure that all vents are open before pumping out otherwise the vacuum created could implode the tank.

Waste water from sinks and showers can go straight into the waterway. Use eco-friendly cleaning products on board that are free from phosphate, chlorine, bleach, and microplastics (Polyethylene).

Do not throw any rubbish overboard. Even organic matter can take a long time to rot down and may be harmful to the wild life. Discarded plastic can cause problems for propellers and sluice gates.

Recycling facilities are available at many marinas - consider taking home "dry rubbish" for recycling.

Dispose of rubbish where you see this sign.

For further information on how to make your inland boating more environmentally sustainable, visit The Green Blue's website at www.thegreenblue.org.uk or contact info@thegreenblue.org.uk. The website includes a wide range of excellent advice and resources, including a handy Pump Out Directory.

Report any pollution or fly-tipping to the Environment Agency on:

FREEPHONE 0800 80 70 60

Do not pump oily water from your boat's bilges into the waterway. Well-maintained engines should not leak oil, but check the bilge sock under the engine and gearbox regularly. Use biodegradable oils, if possible and recycle old oil. To find your nearest oil recycling bank visit www.oilbankline.org.uk.

BOATING AROUND WILDLIFE

Your boat's wash can erode banks, damage plant life and destroy nests and burrows.

If you create a breaking wash, you are going too fast, whatever the speed limit.

The non-towpath side of the canal is often especially rich in flora and fauna.

Do not moor on this side unless there are facilities provided.

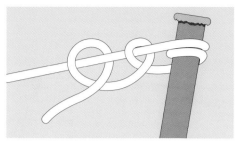

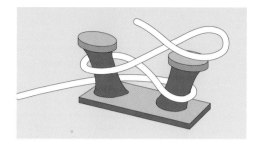

Round turn and two half hitches
Ideal for mooring lines as it can be released under tension. Also used for attaching fenders.

Figure-of-eight
Secure by taking a turn round the back of the cleat, then add at least two figure-of-eight turns for friction.

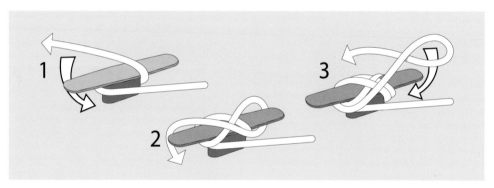

Locking hitch
Take a turn, then make two figure-of-eights over the tee. Finally, make a loop and secure over the horn of the cleat.

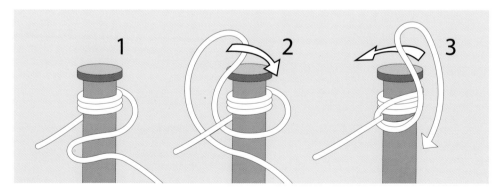

Canalman's hitch
The favourite knot for a narrowboat. The one most used by the old working boatmen as it holds firm but CANNOT lock up. It can even be undone under load. Use for tying up to mooring bollards on the bank or "dollies" aboard. Don't put too many hitches on (three is about right).

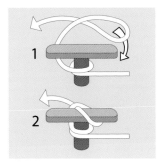

Tee stud hitch

An ideal knot to use with a traditional tee stud. Useful when swigging (below).
You can loosen the hitch quickly by pushing it off the tee with your foot.

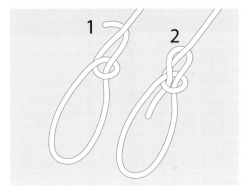

Bowline

Ideal for making a loop to put over a bollard or used as a rescue aid (see p35).
Cannot be undone under load.

Swigging or swaging

With a turn around a cleat, you can tighten (or shorten) the line by pulling on the line whilst holding tension on the cleat, then releasing the line whilst taking up the slack.

For heavier applications, use your body weight – but hold on tightly. Never shorten the line by taking turns over the cleat or tee stud. When it is untied, it will jam.

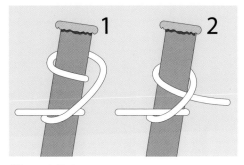

Clove hitch

Easy way to attach a line to a round handrail. Essential when using mooring stakes: if the stake goes into the water, the line will stay attached, making it easy to recover.

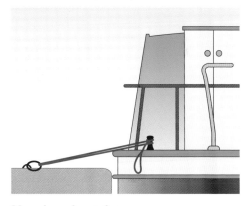

Mooring rings & eyes

Looping a line through a mooring ring and then tying it off back aboard is a good way of securing the boat and a very easy way of releasing the line. When casting off, merely undo the knot and pull the end of the line through the ring to release.

Caution

Always tie the lines off back aboard. Never tie off and leave the rope end lying on the bank. If you do, you can be sure that someone will think it a good idea, late at night, to untie it and set you adrift! Make it difficult for them by hiding the end back aboard! They won't be so keen to climb on the boat!

Handling lines
To join two lines together, use a double sheet bend. Ideal for different diameter ropes.

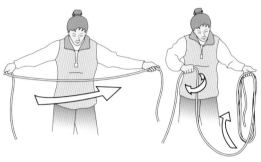

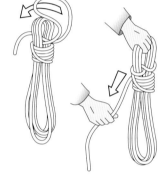

Coiling a line
A regular rhythm of an arm's length creates an even coil. Three strand (laid) rope is coiled clockwise with a right hand twist in each turn. Plaited rope tends to form figure-of-eights.

Both can be stored like this. Always keep lines tidy.

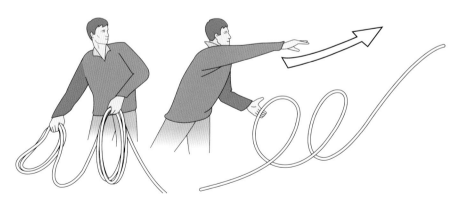

Throwing a line
Coil the line and divide it in two. Swing and throw the end coil while releasing the other. Make sure one end is secure otherwise you will throw the whole line.

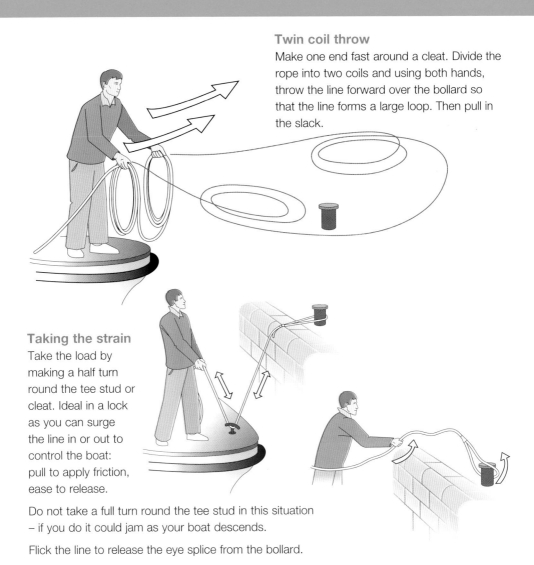

Twin coil throw

Make one end fast around a cleat. Divide the rope into two coils and using both hands, throw the line forward over the bollard so that the line forms a large loop. Then pull in the slack.

Taking the strain

Take the load by making a half turn round the tee stud or cleat. Ideal in a lock as you can surge the line in or out to control the boat: pull to apply friction, ease to release.

Do not take a full turn round the tee stud in this situation – if you do it could jam as your boat descends.

Flick the line to release the eye splice from the bollard.

Centre lines

Most modern narrowboats and some cruisers are fitted with a fixing point (on the cabin roof of a narrowboat or the side decks or roof of a cruiser) to which a handling rope can be fitted. This line is called a "centre line", or on cruisers a "lazy line" or lines, as there may be two, one either side. Kept coiled up on the roof with one end attached to the fixing point, they are used for assisting with boat handling when mooring or going through locks. They are particularly useful to the "single-handed" boater or couple. For more detail see pages 47 and 49.

Centre line

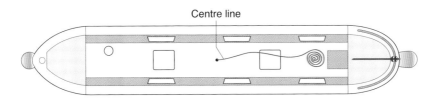

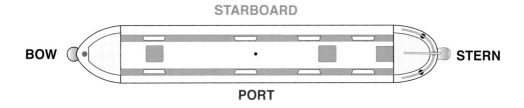

STARBOARD

BOW

STERN

PORT

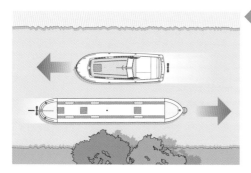

- Keep to the right when passing approaching craft. Port-to-port (left-to-left) is the general rule on all waterways.

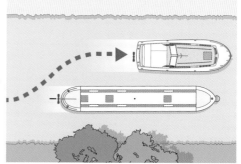

- Overtake on the left. Do not overtake near bridges or bends. Make sure that the other boat knows your intentions.
- If you are overtaking it's your responsibility to keep clear of the other boat.
- If you are the overtaken boat, on canals, which aren't as wide as rivers, you must control when you are ready to be overtaken.

1 Choose a straight section then indicate to the overtaker that you are ready.

2 Move over a few feet to the right and SLOW RIGHT DOWN. As the overtaker passes, your bow first pushes to the right and you nearly come to a halt. Keep the power on slow and keep steering. As they pass your bow returns left and your speed increases again. Be prepared to steer your bow right to avoid hitting their stern.

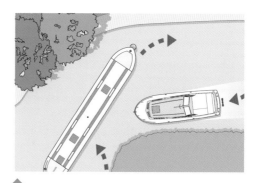

- Large boats may need to swing wide on bends. Wait if you can or sound two short blasts 'I am turning to port' (see page 76) and pass on the wrong side.

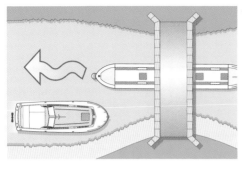

- When approaching a bridge or other narrow section, slow down well in advance.
- If a boat coming the other way is nearer, wave them through first. Keep right until they are clear.
- On rivers, the boat coming downstream is the 'stand-on' vessel. The vessel coming upstream should give way.

The navigation channel on a river is marked by buoys:

Facing upstream: **RED** buoys (can) are on the left.
GREEN buoys (cone) are on the right.

Facing downstream: **RED** buoys are on the right.
GREEN buoys are on the left.

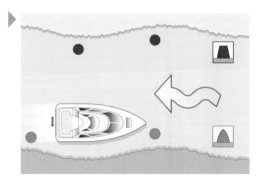

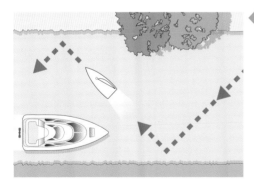

- Sailing boats often need to zigzag (tack) to make progress against the wind.
- When approaching a sailing boat, slow down and wait for an opportunity to pass astern.
- Never cross in front unless you are asked to do so.
- If you get caught up in a boat race, slow down but maintain your course.

Wide rivers often have strong currents especially midstream and on the outside of bends. Boats going upstream can stay close to the edge or the inside of bends where the current is weaker but it may be shallower.

Rowing boats may be using the current to their advantage. As rowers may not see you, use sound signals to show your intentions (see page 76).
On some waters they have right of way.

Controls

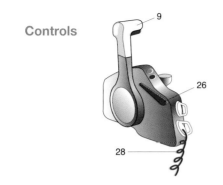

1   fuel tank
2   fuel filler
3   fuel tank vent
4   fuel line
5   fuel filters
6   engine
7   oil dipstick
8   oil filler
9   single lever control
10   cooling water header tank
11   starter battery
12   battery isolater switch
13   stern tube greaser
14   weed hatch
15   propeller
16   gearbox dipstick
17   cooling water intake filter
18   keel cooler
19   stern tube
20   engine hand start
21   gear operating lever
22   transom mounting bracket
23   outboard / outdrive leg
24   cooling water tell tale
25   cooling water inlet grille
26   fast idle control (some controls only)
27   fuel bulb
28   kill cord (always attach this to yourself when engine is running)

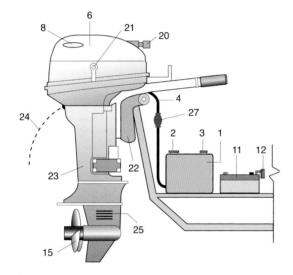

Outboard

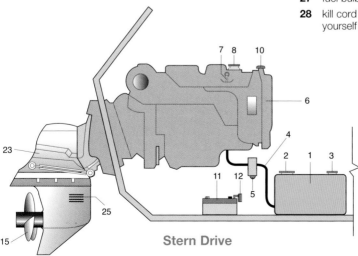

Stern Drive

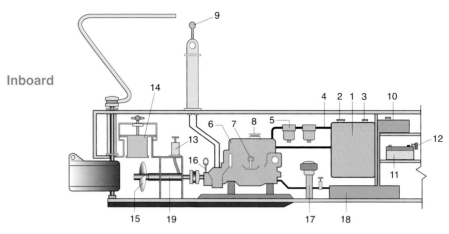

Inboard

Pre-start checks

For both types
- Ensure engine is in neutral
- Check fuel level and fuel is turned to on
- Turn battery isolator on
- Check engine and gearbox oil levels
- Check any drive belts for condition and tension
- Ensure air vent on tank is open

For diesel
- Check stern tube for leaks and use greaser
- Check header tank level
- Check cooling water filters
- Ensure engine stop is returned
- Turn key and hold for a few seconds until the engine starts

For petrol
- If inboard; vent engine bay of any fumes before starting
- Prime fuel system (in an outboard engine) by squeezing bulb
- Engage choke (if needed)
- Some engines require revs in neutral
- Electric start, use starter in short bursts
- Manual start; make sure all crew are clear then give a good solid pull on the cord
- When started check cooling water tell tale
- Return choke knob if used
- Adjust throttle to allow for warm up

Narrowboat weed hatch

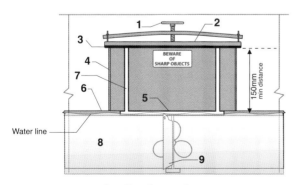

Section from stern

1 Clamp
2 Weed hatch cover
3 Gasket
4 Weed hatch box
5 Splash plate

6 Counter bottom
7 Splash plate supports
8 Swim
9 Rudder

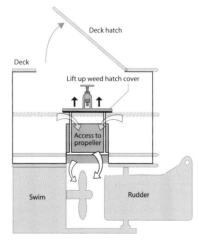

Section through stern

All boats have different handling characteristics so practice is the best way to get to know your boat.

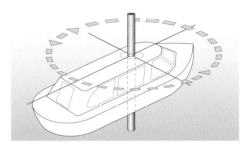

Pivot point

Boats do not steer like cars. Going forwards, they pivot on a point about one third to half way from the bow so allow enough room for the stern to move sideways when turning. (Much like a shopping trolley.)

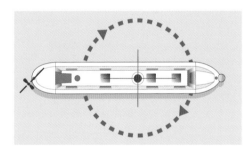

Tiller steering

Push the tiller away from the direction you want to go. Tiller steering from the stern allows you to judge the swing of the bow and position the stern more easily. On most narrowboats, if the engine is in neutral you will not be able to steer. **No gear - no steer!** Always stand in front of the tiller when steering a narrowboat. Don't stand alongside it, because the tiller could swing violently and push you overboard if the rudder was to hit something on the bottom of the canal!

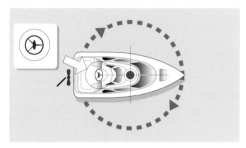

Wheel steering

Turn the wheel in the direction you want to go. Wheel steering is less direct than a tiller and when the wheel is at the front of the boat it is difficult to see what the stern is doing.

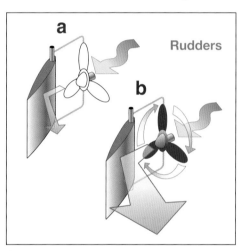

Rudders

a The rudder works by deflecting the water passing over the surface.

On most narrow-boats the rudder has little effect when coasting along in neutral. The same is true for outdrive boats. Some cruisers answer the helm quite well out of gear. Generally the rule is *No Gear = No Steer.*

b When the prop is in forward gear, water passes over the rudder's surface so the boat will steer better. In confined spaces, a short burst of power will increase the rudder's effect without imparting too much additional momentum.

When manoeuvring in confined spaces, a short burst of power will increase steerage without adding too much speed.

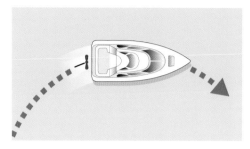
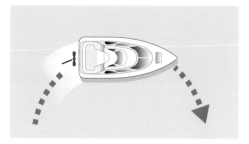

At low revs, the boat will turn slowly in a large arc.

By increasing the revs, the boat will turn more tightly but quicker.

On some narrow boats, 'pumping' the tiller may help you turn in confined spaces. Many boats will slip sideways during a turn. This is aggravated by a crosswind.

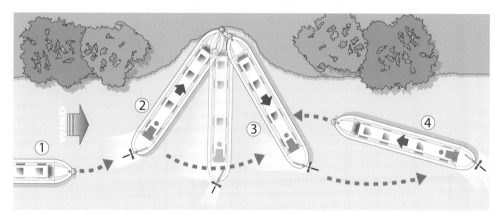

Turning in a winding hole

On canals or narrow rivers, longer boats will need to use a winding hole.

- Always put the bow into the winding hole never the stern, otherwise you will damage the prop.
- Push the tiller over and start turning into the winding hole.
- Glide gently up to the deepest part, applying reverse to stop with the bows resting gently on the bank.

- Now apply revs in forward gear with the tiller pointing the way you want to go.
- The stern will motor across to the other side of the winding hole.
- Push the tiller the other way and reverse off until you are clear. As before, if you can use prop effect it will help you turn. (see page 30).

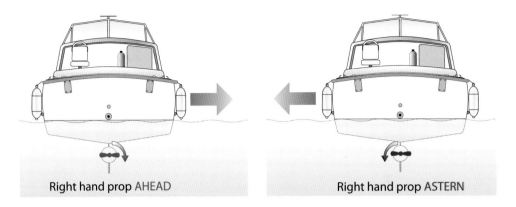

Right hand prop AHEAD   Right hand prop ASTERN

Propeller effect

This affects the stern as that is where the propeller is situated. More commonly referred to as "Paddle wheel" effect, "prop walk" or "transverse thrust", it pushes the stern sideways. Think of the prop as a paddle wheel. A right-handed prop rotates clockwise (when seen from behind as in the picture) when ahead gear is engaged, pushing the stern to starboard (right). When in reverse it rotates anti-clockwise, and "paddle wheels" the stern to port (left). Vice versa for a left-handed prop. We can control this effect in forward gear by applying a little opposite rudder. In reverse, however the rudder has little effect on it.

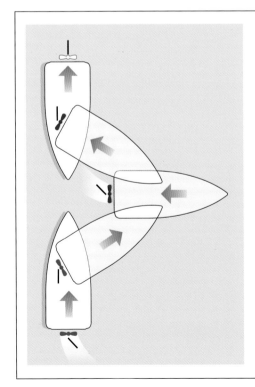

Ideal three-point turn

If the boat has a right-handed propeller, the stern will kick to port when you go astern, giving you much more help than the rudder.

- In a very narrow channel you might have to go ahead and astern several times.
- The secret of efficient turning in a limited space is always to steer the tiller/put the helm over THEN apply the power.

Turning 180 degrees

Choose your turning direction to take advantage of prop effect, wind and current.

- Put the helm over, burst of revs ahead to start the turn, into neutral.
- Then apply opposite helm and give a burst astern to keep her turning with prop effect, into neutral.
- Apply opposite helm again and go ahead to bring her round.

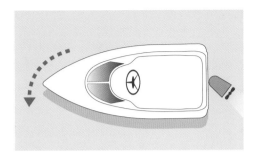

Outboards

Although some outboards have an add-on rudder to improve slow speed manoeuvring, most can only steer the boat when the propeller is driving.

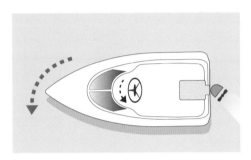

Outdrives and sterndrives

These steer like an outboard but the engine is inside the boat. Much sharper turns can be achieved in both directions than with a conventional prop and rudder system.

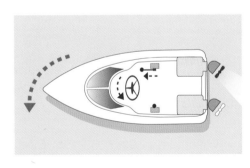

Twin outdrives

With twin outdrives the outside one will have greater leverage than the inside one.

So, to turn left: wheel to the left and power on right engine. Opposite to turn right.

Outboards, outdrives and sterndrives all have a common theme:

- Engine to neutral / steer the leg / apply the power.
- This gives maximum manoeuvrability / minimum speed.

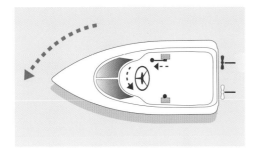

Twin props

As the propellers are offset from the centre line of the boat, by running just one you can turn the boat without using the rudders.

To make a tighter turn, use the rudders as well.

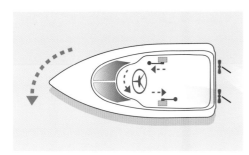

For a really tight turn, put the rudders hard over and go ahead on one engine and astern with the other. The combined effect will turn the boat in its own length.

Use power in short bursts (tickover is often sufficient) to stop speed and momentum building up.

Most inland waterway boats do not steer well in reverse so it takes practice.

Tiller steering
- Make allowances for the wind.
- On narrow canals, keep the boat in the centre of the channel.
- Once central, look astern and point the rudder in the direction you want to go.
- Apply as little power as possible. Too much and the tiller will swing around violently.
- Keep glancing forward to check the swing of the bow. As the pivot point moves further back when reversing, the bow swing will be greater, giving you a vital clue as to where the boat is heading.

- If the bow is swinging the wrong way, point the rudder in the opposite direction and apply a burst of ahead (forward) power to correct it.
- If you have a bowthruster then use it in conjunction with the rudder to keep the bow central in the channel. If it is an electric one, use it in short bursts only. **NEVER** use it in shallow water, otherwise you might damage it!

Wheel steering
- Look astern and turn the wheel in the direction you want the stern to go. Continually check the bow swing and alter the wheel position accordingly.
- Use as little power as possible.
- Use neutral to stop momentum building up.

On twin-engine boats, use alternate engines to keep the speed down.

On canals

- If someone falls overboard, think before you act. Do not jump in yourself or let anyone else do so.
- Put the engine into neutral to stop the prop.

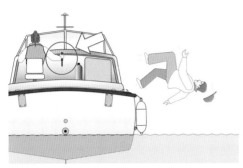

- Do not reverse back to the MOB, they could get sucked into the prop.
- Throw a lifebelt to the MOB.

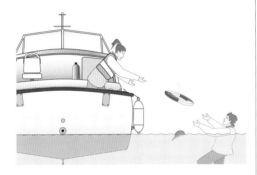

- Tell them to try and stand up. Canals are quite shallow, especially at the edges, so they may be able to wade to the bank.
- Head the boat for the bank and get someone off the boat to help the MOB climb out of the water.

On wide rivers and deeper canals

If the MOB cannot stand up:
- Throw a lifebelt to the MOB.
- Proceed past the MOB, keeping the boat's stern well away from them.
- Turn the boat round and approach the MOB very slowly up into the current.

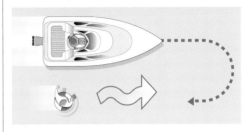

- Put the engine in neutral. You and the MOB will both drift at the same speed on a river.

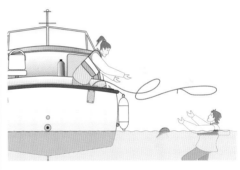

- Throw the MOB a line with a large bowline at the end (see page 21).
- Tell the MOB to put the rope over his head and under his armpits.
- Pull the MOB to the side of the boat and help them aboard.

In any MOB situation you need to act quickly. If you go through the drill with the crew before you set off, everyone will know what to do and when. Make sure that all the crew know where the safety equipment is kept and know how to use it.

Weil's disease

Although the risk of infection is small, it is sensible to take the following precautions after falling in:
• Take a shower • Wash all cuts and abrasions and treat with a sterile dressing • Wash wet clothing thoroughly before further use • If flu-like symptoms develop within two weeks, see a doctor. Tell him that you fell in the canal/river.

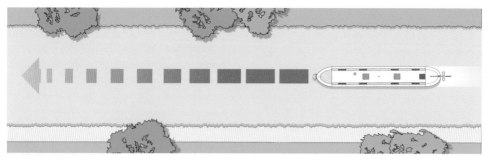

Boats do not have brakes and will travel quite a long way after you take the engine out of gear. Even if you go into reverse, the momentum will still carry the boat forward for a while. So slow down early, ease off the throttle to tick over in forward gear and only use reverse to come to a final stop. Remember, many boats do not steer well in neutral.

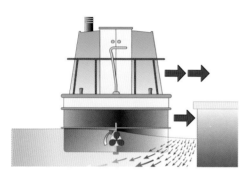 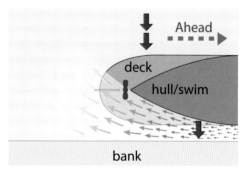

Bank effect or interaction

If you go too fast, too close to the bank, the prop will draw the water between you and the bank down and your stern will get sucked sideways towards it. This will seriously affect your steering! It also happens if you go too fast, too close to another boat. This is called interaction, so slow down when passing or overtaking.

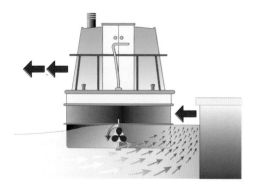 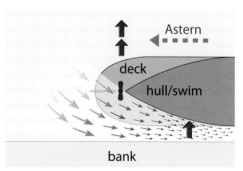

Reverse bank effect

When approaching the bank to stop, going into reverse with a narrowboat can force the stern away from the bank because the prop-wash is forced forwards along between the hull and the bank. To avoid it happening, try engaging reverse and almost stopping the boat with the stern further away from the bank, then putting the tiller over towards the bank and giving a brief surge of forward, then neutral, to swing the stern in under its own momentum.

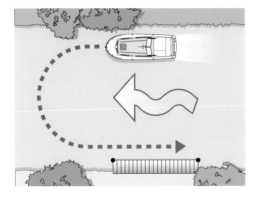

Using the current to help you stop

On rivers it is much easier to stop by turning around and heading into the current. It is also easier to moor this way round. Plus, your propeller(s) will not be fouled by debris floating downstream.

Always look behind you before turning to check that the way is clear – use correct sound signals (see page 76).

Allow plenty of room if turning downstream. The current may carry you further than you anticipate. Note: currents can speed up dramatically near weirs and bridges. Be cautious turning upstream of bridges.

Speed over ground

On rivers, the current will affect your speed over the ground.

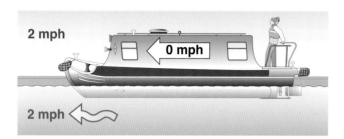

Going downstream, even without power, you will travel at the current's speed of 2 mph.

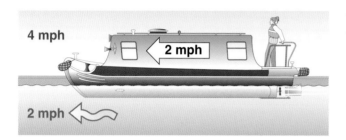

With the engine pushing the boat through the water at 2 mph plus the current's speed of 2 mph you will be moving at a combined speed of 4 mph.

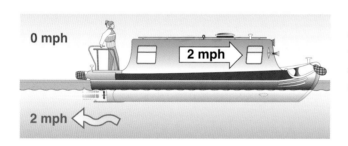

Heading upstream, the boat will need to make 2 mph through the water just to stand still against the 2 mph current.

STRONG CURRENTS

Although canals are normally pond-like, rivers may have strong currents. This can make boat handling interesting and good judgement is required.

- Make sure that your boat has enough power to cope with the flow of the river. If not, tie up and wait for a change in the strength of the current.
- Keep an anchor and chain ready to deploy at the upstream end of the boat. This is your emergency brake and is one of the Boat Safety Scheme requirements. Make sure the rope & chain is well secured to the anchorage point!

- Check local information and obey warning signs.
- Keep well clear of weirs – watch out for warning signs.
- Make sure you are familiar with the Navigation Authority's "Strong Stream" warning system. Don't cruise when the warnings are in place - seek a safe mooring and wait for the stream to abate.

Crosswinds can have a serious effect, so always be aware of where the wind is coming from.

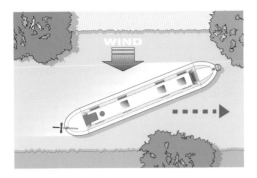

If there is a crosswind, adopt a 'crab-like' position, steering the bow into the wind.

The stronger the crosswind, the greater the angle.

Keep the stern in deep water to gain maximum push from the prop.

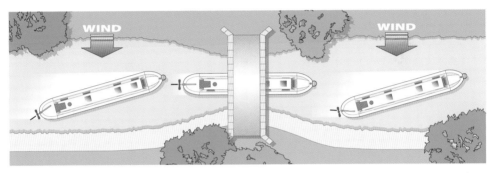

Straighten up to go through bridges. Once through, increase the engine revs and resume the 'crab' position as soon as possible.

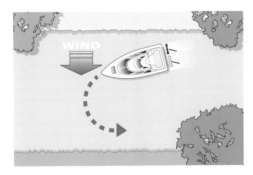

Use the wind to help you turn round. Turning away from the wind (downwind) can help to push the bow round on some boats.

On a narrowboat, however, it may just push you sideways so turn into the wind if possible.

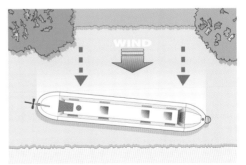

You can harness a crosswind to gently push you onto or off the bank. However, be aware of sudden gusts of wind.

You can see the wind by ripples on the water, flying flags, moving trees and bushes.

On all canals the maximum speed is 4 mph (fast walking pace). On shallow waterways you may need to travel much slower. On rivers, where the water is deeper and the channel wider, speed limits vary between 5 – 8 mph depending on whether you are going up or downstream. Check local regulations. The golden rule for speed is "Look behind, don't make waves!" If you are making a breaking stern wash that's too fast – slow down a bit!

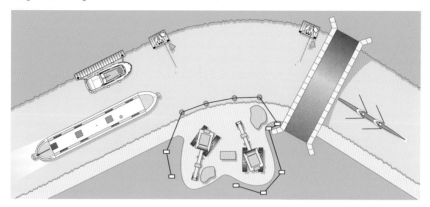

Slow down when:

- You are making a breaking wave along the bank.
- Passing moored craft, rowers or anglers.
- Passing engineering works. Look for which side to pass – green or white markers.
- Negotiating blind bends – but slow down early, not as you are turning otherwise you will lose your steering.
- Passing through narrow bridges, over aqueducts, entering tunnels or anywhere else with a channel restriction.
- If in doubt, slow down, or stop, and assess the situation before proceeding.

Bottom effect

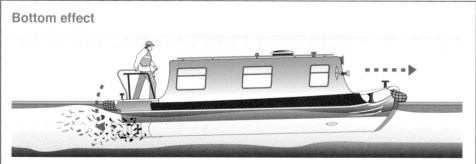

In shallow water you probably won't go any faster by opening up the throttle. All this will do is suck the stern down and disturb bottom debris, which will become entangled in the prop and can even severely damage it.

You may encounter all sorts of floating rubbish, especially under bridges. As you approach, speed up and then reduce to tick over (or neutral if it is really bad) and glide through. This way, you will not foul your prop.

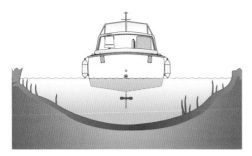

Canals are generally saucer shaped and deeper in the middle.

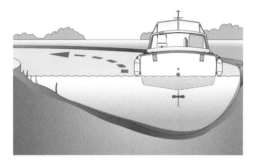

Bends on rivers are generally deeper towards the outside where the current has "scoured out" the channel.

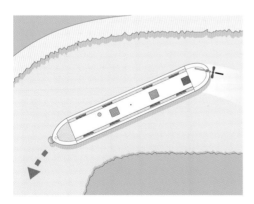

On tight bends you may have to put the helm over and give bursts of forward throttle to get the boat to swing round. Do not cut the corner – or you may run aground.

GOING AGROUND

If you go aground going forwards, you should be able to reverse off.

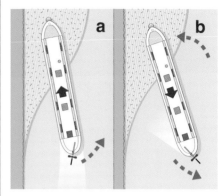

Do not try to turn the bow away from the bank.

(a) First, turn the bow in towards the bank to put the stern in deeper water.

(b) Now reverse off.

If that does not work, position the crew along the side of the boat away from the shallows and try to reverse again. Rocking the boat sometimes helps.

Use the pole to keep the stern in deep water or to push the fore end off. Place the pole firmly on the bank so it won't slip. Hold the pole to the side of you. Do not use the pole as a lever, it will only break.

If all this fails, try emptying your water tank(s), this will lighten the bow.

You could always ask a passing boat to tow you off. If you do, make sure that they use your rope, and that you double it up for added strength.

As many river banks are privately owned, finding an overnight river mooring can sometimes be a problem. However, there will be public moorings available, usually in riverside towns and villages. Most cruising guides show the public mooring sites.

Popular moorings fill up quickly, so you may need to arrive early to find space or be prepared to double up with other craft.

On canals the situation is easier, mooring along the towpath is normally free for up to 14 days in one place.

The picture illustrates prohibited areas.

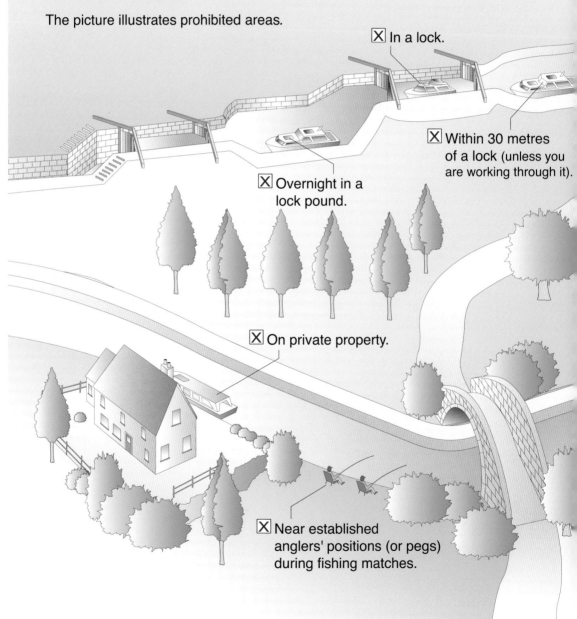

X In a lock.

X Within 30 metres of a lock (unless you are working through it).

X Overnight in a lock pound.

X On private property.

X Near established anglers' positions (or pegs) during fishing matches.

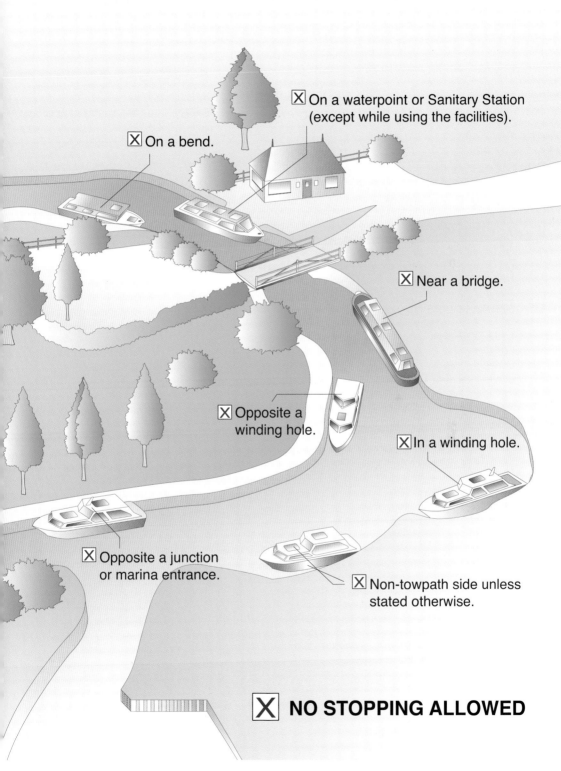

X On a bend.

X On a waterpoint or Sanitary Station (except while using the facilities).

X Near a bridge.

X Opposite a winding hole.

X In a winding hole.

X Opposite a junction or marina entrance.

X Non-towpath side unless stated otherwise.

X **NO STOPPING ALLOWED**

On a river, always moor with your bow facing upstream into the current.

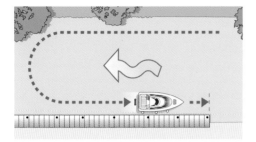

If cruising downstream, you will need to turn your boat:

- Before you turn, brief your crew and have mooring lines and fenders ready.
- Proceed downstream past the mooring, then check that the river is clear of traffic.
- Turn round smartly into the current.
- Move upstream to the pontoon, stopping at the top end (to allow others to moor behind you).

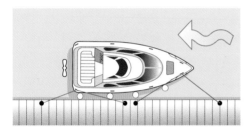

- Secure the bow first, then the stern line.
- Position the fenders in the correct place.
- Use spring lines if the boat is surging back and forth in the current or the wash of other boats.
- If you are mooring on a river overnight, leave some slack in the mooring lines to allow for a fall or rise in the water level.
- If you are mooring on a tidal river, make sure you will have enough water at low tide.

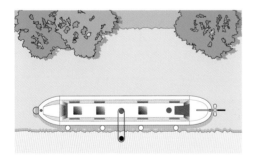

- On both rivers and canals using a centre line, (or "lazy line" on rivers) for a temporary mooring is very popular, particularly when there are just one or two in the crew. See page 47 for the "coming alongside" procedure. Once ashore with the line, pull the boat to a halt and then secure it to a bollard using the "canalman's hitch" (see page 20) or take it through a mooring ring and secure back to the centre line cleat aboard. This rope can also be used in locks to hold the boat steady, but not in large river locks where the turbulence is too great.

On most visitor and permanent mooring sites there are rings or bollards to moor to. At other locations you should use the mooring pins (stakes) and hammer or the piling hooks carried aboard.

Mooring Stakes

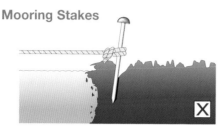

- Drive the stakes in at an angle away from the boat, to about three quarters of their length. Don't put them too near the edge!

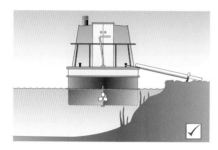

- If your boat is not directly against the bank, use your gang plank – avoid jumping on or off the boat.

- Never stretch your mooring lines across the towpath, it could cause an accident.
- Avoid tying lines around trees, they can wear through the bark and kill the tree.
- At a popular mooring, move up close to the next boat rather than leave a gap.
- Be prepared to move up to accommodate other arrivals.
- If necessary, double up at popular places - always ask first.

- Place an empty plastic bottle or plastic carrier bag over the stake, to prevent passers-by tripping up.

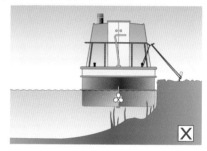

- Don't pass the rope over the pulpit or stern rail. Take it from the cleat, through the fairlead (if you have one) and to the stake.
- Tie a clove hitch around the stake, then pass the rope back aboard, tying off on the cleat or dolly.
- Coil any spare rope up and stow it neatly.
- Remember to put the hammer back on board.

Piling Hooks

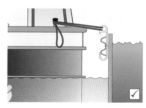 

When you want to moor to a piled bank, a very good alternative to mooring stakes are piling hooks. These provide a more secure hold, are easier to use, and don't require a hammer! They work by being passed down between the "waling" (that's the horizontal "Armco" type railing) and the piling, twisted 90 degrees and then pulled up against the rail. Make very sure that you attach the mooring rope first before insertion otherwise if you let the hook slip, you will lose it in the water!

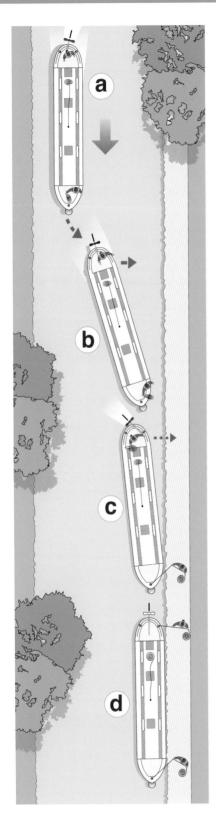

ARRIVING

Needs two people

(**a**) Slow down well ahead of your intended mooring spot, but keep in slow ahead – don't go into neutral. Brief your crew. Attach the stern line to the dolly and get one crew member to go forward to prepare the bow line.

(**b**) Turn into the bank and use reverse gently to stop as the bow reaches the bank. Put engine in neutral. The crew steps ashore with the bow line. Allow plenty of slack – do not pull the rope.

(**c**) Start the stern swinging in by pushing the tiller hard over towards the bank and using a burst of forward power, then a quick burst of reverse (to stop forward motion), then into neutral and let the stern slide alongside.

(**d**) Step off the stern with stern rope, (or hand to a crew member) and then both ropes are pulled at the same time to hold the boat in. Tie bow and stern to bollards or pins.

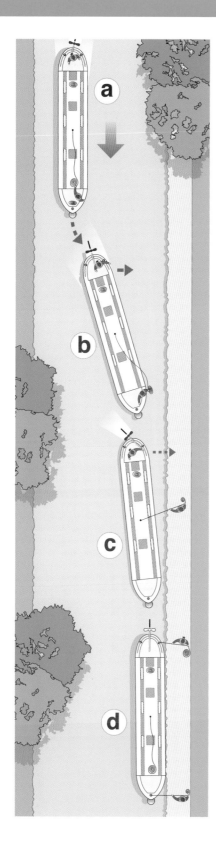

Mooring alongside using a centre line

Needs two people

- An easier method when there are only one or two crew is to bring the boat alongside with just the one centre line. See page 23 for details of this rope.
- Use the same procedure as in (a) but using the centre line instead of the bow and stern lines.
- Run the line forward to the front of the cabin roof.
- In (b), as the bow reaches the bank, the crew steps ashore with the line.
- In (c), the crew then pull on the line to bring the boat alongside. Don't put the line round a bollard if the boat is still moving because if the line jams this will arrest the movement of the boat so quickly that it will heel over violently!
- If you are staying for more than a short time rig the bow and stern lines and then coil and stow the centre line back on the roof.

Mooring alongside – single handed – with centre line

- Use the same procedure as in (a) and (b), but have the centre line run to the rear of the cabin roof near the steerer.
- Engage forward gear as in (c) to swing the stern in to the bank.
- Steerer steps off the stern with the centre line and pulls the boat in to the bank, engine in neutral.

LEAVING

Needs two people

(a) Start the engine in neutral. Check for approaching craft. Be aware of the wind direction; is it blowing in towards the bank or away from it? On the bow or the stern? Brief the crew to untie the bow line, coil it but on no account let it go otherwise the wind will blow the boat away! Withdraw the stake or remove the piling hook and stow aboard. Do the same with the stern line, stake etc. Have a final check to make sure that all stakes, hooks and the mooring hammer are stowed aboard.

(b) When you are ready, the bow crew puts the line on board then, still standing on the bank, pushes the bow out into the channel, remaining on the bank. They then walk to the stern and board the boat, take the stern line from the stern crew, coil it up and stow it on the cabin roof or somewhere else clear of the deck. (Hanging it from the tiller pin is not recommended!)

(c) Then the stern crew push the stern clear of the bank as they get aboard, holding on to the handrails, one foot on the boat and the other on the bank. It's much easier and safer to board from the stern than the bow on most narrowboats.

(d) Once clear engage forward gear and get up to cruising speed. (As quickly as possible if there is a side wind blowing).

Remember that if you use too many revs too close to the bank this will have the effect of holding the stern into the bank! (Interaction – bank effect – see page 36).

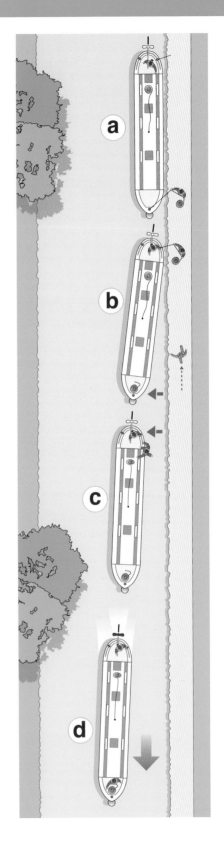

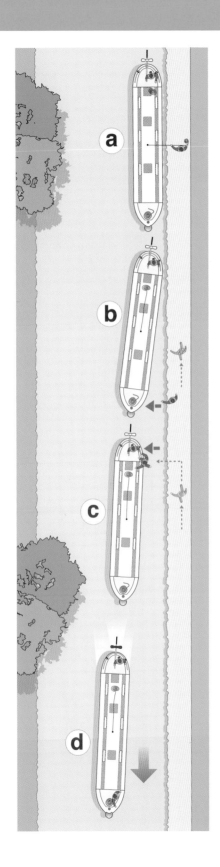

Leaving a mooring using a centre line

(**a**) While one crew member stands on the bank and holds the boat steady using the centre line held at right angles to the boat, the other crew untie the bow and stern lines, board the boat and stow the lines etc.

(**b**) When ready to go the centre line crew stows the line on the front of the cabin roof, pushes the bow out, then walks to the stern.

(**c**) Then the crew push that clear as they get aboard.

(**d**) Once clear engage forward gear and get up to cruising speed.

Leaving a mooring - single handed - with centre line

Using the same procedure as above, after stowing the mooring lines, the single hander unties the centre line and stows it on the roof. They then walk forward and push the bows clear, then board at the stern, pushing this clear as they step on board.

You must ensure that both bow and stern are clear of the bank, and crew are aboard before engaging gear.

Don't just drive away from the bank or you may damage the prop.

Always push out into deeper water, using the pole if necessary.

You may need to use the boat pole to hold the boat clear if there is a strong side wind blowing.

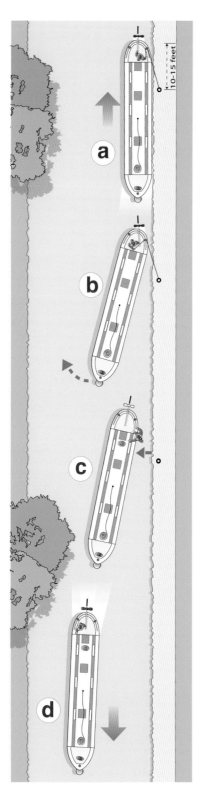

Narrowboat "springing off" a mooring.

A useful technique if you are a solo crew and a strong wind is holding the boat in to the mooring.

(**a**) Untie the bow line and stow aboard. Then loosen the stern line from the cleat and reverse the boat so that the stern line runs forward for about 10 – 15 feet. Re-attach the line or take a turn round the cleat and hold it firmly in your hand. Ensure that you are aboard.

(**b**) Engage reverse gear and hold the stern line. Increase the revs until the bow starts swinging clear of the bank.

(**c**) When the bow is at 45 degrees or more to the bank engage neutral, disconnect the stern line and pull aboard,

(**d**) Then engage forward and motor away. Simple and effective!

This technique can only be used where you are moored to a bollard, mooring ring or other bank side fixture.

Ensure that there is enough depth of water at the bank so that the prop does not foul the bottom.

Remember: it is always easier to moor heading into the current (or wind if it is stronger).

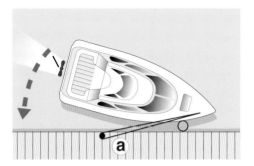

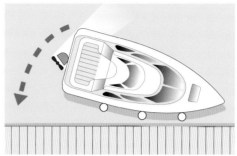

Single prop

- If space is tight or there's a strong wind, use a spring line **(a)**.
- Approach at a wide angle to the bank and secure the spring to a bollard.
- With a big fender at the bow, turn the rudder away from the bank and motor slowly ahead.
- The boat can't go forward, so it will swing into the bank.

Single sterndrive

- Same procedure as single prop, if the gap is tight. If you have more room, just motor in at a gentle angle and put the engine into neutral.
- Then turn the helm towards the bank and apply astern power to pull the stern in.

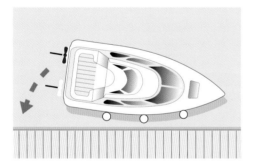

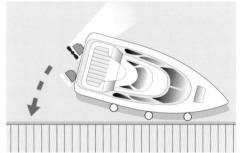

Twin props

Again, a spring can be used in a tight space but with practice the engines alone will get you in. If tick-over on both engines is too fast, use just the outside engine. As you glide up to your chosen spot in neutral, put the outside engine in astern. This will swing the stern in.

Twin sterndrives

Use the same approach as twin props. Put the engines into neutral and see how it glides in. When alongside, turn the wheel towards the bank and engage astern on the outside engine.

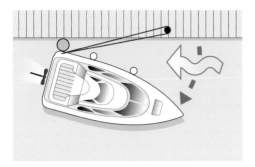

Single prop

If there's a strong current but not much room – rig a line from the stern, around a bollard and back to the boat. Release the bow and let the water flow push it out. Slip the line and motor away.

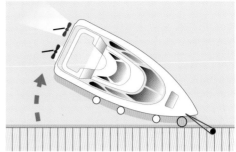

Twin props

Protect the bow with fenders and go astern on the inside prop. If there's a strong wind you might need a touch of ahead from the outside prop or a bow line to pull against.

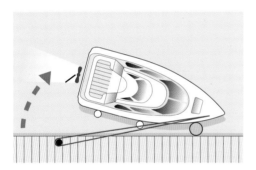

If there's a strong wind and no current, rig the line at the bow and motor against it to swing the stern out. Always use large fenders to protect the boat.

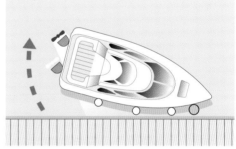

Twin sterndrives

Here is a case for not using opposite helm and engine. Turn the helm to the left and put the left engine in astern. This tends to lift the boat away from the side.

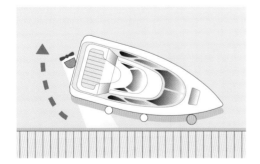

If shallow, to avoid prop damage, use only the outside engine to gently drive her clear.

Single sterndrive

Use a spring in a tight space. Otherwise, turn the prop away from the bank, engage reverse and let it lift you off the bank as you back out.

What are they for?

There were two main reasons for building locks.

(a) Canal locks. These were built to enable canal boats to go up and down hills.

(b) River locks. These were built as our natural rivers were improved over the centuries, to hold back the water and therefore deepen the channel and slow the current. This made it possible for larger craft to navigate further inland.

How do they work?

A lock is simply a chamber, a box of water, with gates at either end. Although there are many types, they all basically work in the same way. By raising or lowering the water level in this "box" you can go up or down hill. Simple!

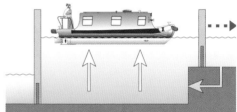

- To go uphill, empty the lock so the level is the same as your vessel.
- Open the gates.
- Enter the lock.
- Close the gates behind you.

- Fill the lock by opening the appropriate sluices.
- When the water level is the same as the one you are moving to, open the gates.
- Exit the lock. Your boat has gone up a level.

Safety at locks

Working the locks is part of the fun of a waterways holiday but it is important to follow a few safety tips:

- When approaching a lock, never jump off the boat. Surfaces can be slippery and a fall between the boat and lock wall could be extremely dangerous.
- Always have a competent person on board.
- Never leave the boat unattended.
- Take your time – don't rush. Keep an eye open for problems.
- Make sure no one has their hands or feet dangling over the boat's side.

- Children should wear lifejackets/ buoyancy aids, be fully supervised and kept well away from the edge.
- Ensure nobody is standing on the wrong side of the balance beam when the gates are being opened. Push gates open, it's easier than pulling.
- When the water rushes in, it can be very noisy. Use hand communication signals which everyone knows beforehand.
- Keep the boat well away from the gates and cills.
- Make sure that the fenders do not get caught on anything.

Types of lock

Locks come in many forms and different sizes to suit the terrain and the job they have to do. We will look at other derivatives later on in this section. These are the three main ones.

Narrow canal lock

A narrow canal is defined as such by the size of its locks. Most are just seven feet wide and 72 feet long. These narrow-locked waterways make up the great majority of our canal system, explaining why most canal boats are narrow beam. Their design follows a fairly standard pattern, so when you master their operation, you master the operation of the majority of locks!

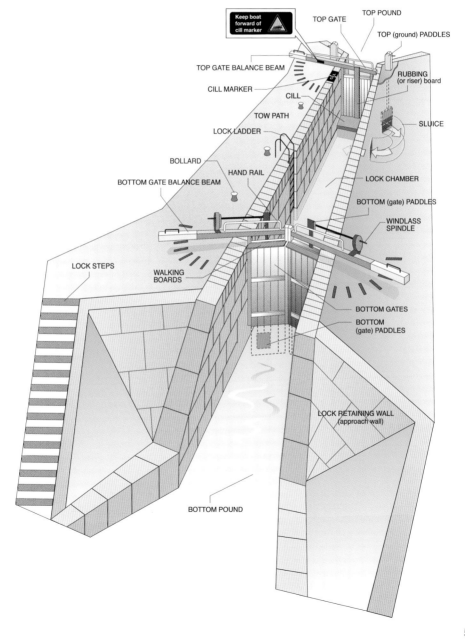

Keep boat forward of cill marker

TOP POUND

TOP GATE

TOP (ground) PADDLES

TOP GATE BALANCE BEAM

RUBBING (or riser) board

CILL MARKER

CILL

TOW PATH

SLUICE

LOCK LADDER

BOLLARD

HAND RAIL

LOCK CHAMBER

BOTTOM GATE BALANCE BEAM

BOTTOM (gate) PADDLES

WINDLASS SPINDLE

LOCK STEPS

WALKING BOARDS

BOTTOM GATES

BOTTOM (gate) PADDLES

LOCK RETAINING WALL (approach wall)

BOTTOM POUND

TYPES OF LOCKS

Broad canal lock

Our broad canals were built wider to take barge traffic rather than narrowboats and so their locks were wider too. Typically 14 – 15 feet wide and 72 feet long. On a few Northern canals, however, although the same width, they were not built as long as that, some are only 58 feet long.

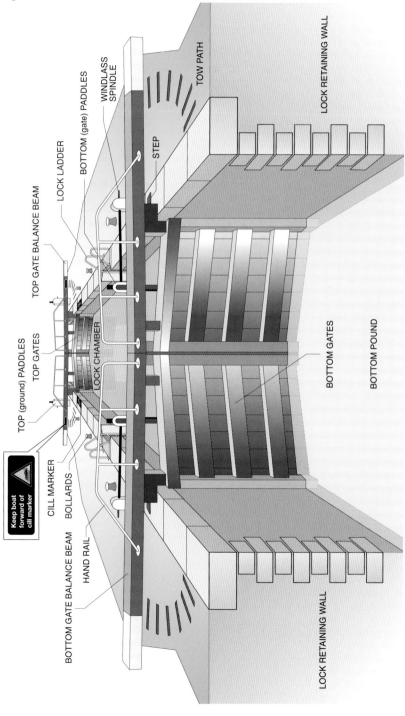

River lock

Most of our smaller rivers were "canalised" over the years and their locks resemble the Broad canal lock pattern, both in appearance and operation. On our larger rivers, however, engineers developed their own unique styles of lock. Some are over 250 feet long and 26 feet wide. These are power operated and have resident lock keepers to control the lock's operation.

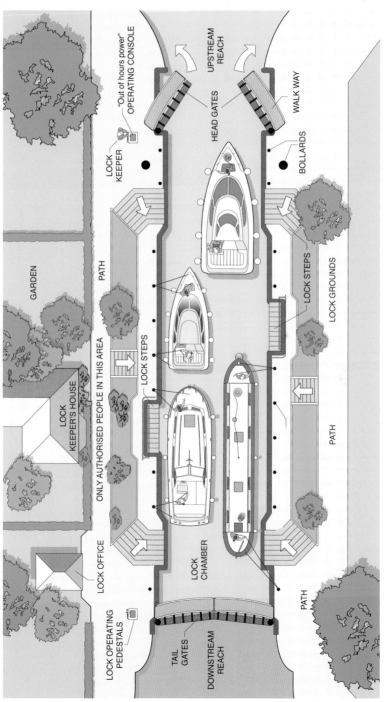

Lock operation – Paddle gear

To work the first two (manual) lock types you will need some special 'tools'.

(a) A windlass (lock key) to wind up the paddle gear which opens the 'paddles' or sluices that let water into or out of the lock. This gear will be either mechanical (rack & pinion) or hydraulic.

(b) An 'anti-vandal' key to unlock some paddle gear. A sign of the times, these paddles are usually to be found in large towns and cities.

(c) A C&RT (Canal & River Trust) 'Watermate' key. Rarely needed on manual paddle gear but common on power operated locks. Make sure that you keep the two keys on floating key rings!

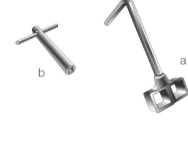

Safe operation of paddle gear

1 Make sure that the safety catch is in place before winding the windlass.

2 Check that the windlass is on the spindle properly. There is:

(a) a parallel spindle on hydraulic paddles.
(b) a tapered spindle on mechanical types.

3 Wind the paddles up slowly but firmly. Never open more than a third initially, especially if the lock only has gate paddles. Then assess water flow before opening further.

4 Remove the windlass from the spindle after winding otherwise it may spin off at dangerously high speed. (No safety catches are necessary on hydraulic paddles).

5 Keep fingers, hair and clothing away from the paddle gearing.

6 Always wind the paddle back down. If you let it drop it may shatter.

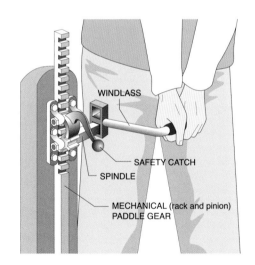

There are two main types of paddle:

Gate paddle (a)
A sliding shutter over an underwater hole in the gate which, when raised, allows water to flow through.

Ground paddle (b)
A shutter in a pipe (culvert) in the ground which, when raised, allows water to flow through.

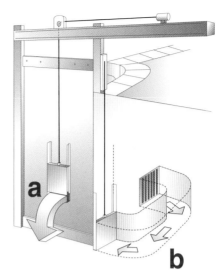

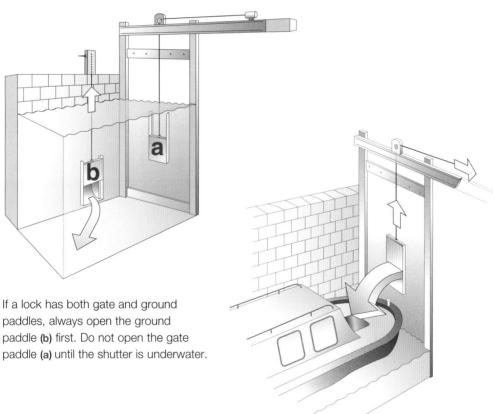

If a lock has both gate and ground paddles, always open the ground paddle (b) first. Do not open the gate paddle (a) until the shutter is underwater.

If you open the gate paddle first, you could flood your boat!

If someone falls into a lock you need to act quickly:

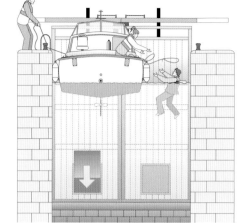

- Stop the engine.

- Close all the paddles.

- Throw a line or lifebelt to the MOB.

- Do not jump in or there are two people to rescue!

- Make sure that the boat cannot swing across and crush the MOB.

- Now consider the best way to get them out.

- Try to get the MOB to the ladder in the wall (all locks have them).

- All vessels should have a boarding ladder.

- If the MOB cannot climb out, you may need to slowly fill the lock to bring him up to your level.

- On many rivers there are lock keepers who are trained in rescue techniques. Always follow their instructions and assist as required.

Lock etiquette. A few pointers to politeness.

- Upon arrival at a lock and finding other boats waiting, make sure that you don't inadvertently queue jump! If you are second in the queue for a lock, consider offering to help the boat in front, especially if they are on their own. Always make sure you ask if they want help, don't just wade in. Sometimes people will want to do it alone. By the same token, don't offer unsolicited advice, as this can upset people!
- When it is your turn, check which way the lock is set; if it's not in your favour and there is a boat heading towards you, then let that boat go through before emptying the lock for yourself.
- If you are sharing a lock with another boat, put the lighter boat behind. This has nothing to do with queue jumping, it's simply that it minimises the risk of damage, particularly if you have a GRP and a steel boat in together.
- On leaving the lock, ensure that you close all the gates and paddles, unless of course there is a boat coming the other way, in which case leave the gate open.

River lock etiquette

1. When you arrive at the lay-by, move right along so that other boats can wait behind, and then turn off your engine.

2. Even if you are first in the queue, the lock keeper will not necessarily call you in first, so be sure to wait until he calls or signals you in.

3. Don't rush into the lock as there might be a boat coming out that you haven't seen. Always wait for the lock keeper's signal.

4. You should use bow and stern lines to secure your boat, as lock keepers will not let you through using a centre line only.

5. Once the boat is held securely, turn your engine off.

6. When exiting the lock, ensure the gates are fully open before leaving.

Working locks requires team work

SAFETY GAP

Going uphill

- As you approach a lock, drop a crew member off to go ahead and get the lock ready. If a boat is approaching downhill, they have priority if the lock is full.
- If the lock is empty, open the bottom gates and steer the boat straight in.
- If the lock is full, moor up far enough away to avoid the turbulence whilst the lock empties.

- If possible, **hold** a line around a bollard or cleat onboard not just in your hand. Do not tie off onto bollard.
- Make sure that the top gates and paddles are closed.
- Open the bottom paddles. Make sure that steerer and lock crew maintain eye contact at all times.
- Now follow for narrow or broad locks.

Narrow canal locks - going uphill

Be aware that the Canal & River Trust have recently installed three bollards along the 'lock ladder' side of all narrow locks where before there were none. Whilst these could be useful if you have a cruiser, they are not usually necessary for a narrowboat.

- Once in the lock, close the bottom gates and paddles.
- If on a cruiser, position the boat centrally in the chamber and pass bow and stern ropes up and around the bollards but do not tie them off. You could use the 'lazy line' here instead.
- If on a narrowboat motor forward gently towards the top cill.
- Check that the cill has fendering and the top gate has a 'riser board'. All narrow locks should have fendering and a riser board fitted, but some may be damaged or otherwise un-usable, or missing! If this is the case then you will need to use a rope to keep the bow clear of the top gate. The centre line is best for this. If the lock has bollards pass the rope up and around one but do not tie it off!

- If the cill fendering and riser board is O.K., rest the bow against the cill and keep your engine going slowly in forward gear to keep it there. You will not normally need to use any ropes. Apply more revs to overcome any excessive initial inrush of water.
- Check that the bottom gates have not inadvertently swung open again, then wind one top ground paddle up a couple of turns, pause, check the inflow of water, then wind another couple of turns, pause, and then continue until the paddle is fully raised. Cross the lock and repeat for the other paddle. If there is a gate paddle then open this last, once the water level is above the paddle hole in the gate. If the paddles are opened too quickly the inrush of water will push the boat back then draw it forward violently! The deeper the lock, the worse the effect! Take your time. Remember to engage the paddle safety catches and remove your windlass.
- When the lock is full, open the gate THEN close the paddles and motor out. Stop and close the gate, unless there is another boat coming the other way.

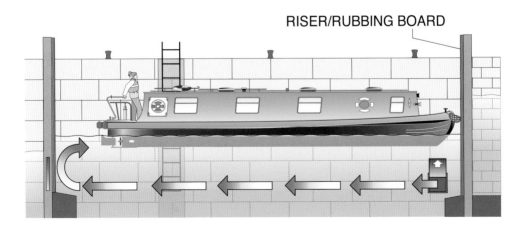

RISER/RUBBING BOARD

Broad canal locks - going uphill

Broad canal locks can usually accommodate two narrow beam boats side-by-side (breasted up) or one wider boat. These locks often have cill fendering but no riser boards and so you will need to keep the bows clear of the top gates. They are equipped with bollards and lock ladders on both sides.

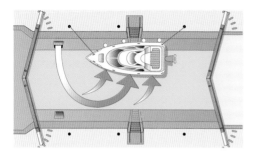
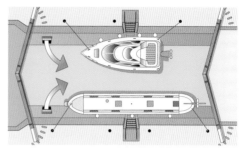

- Once in the lock, close the bottom gates and paddles. If you are the only boat working through, hold the boat to the towpath side (it's easier) and pass bow and stern lines up and around the bollards (don't tie them off!) Cruisers and shorter narrowboats up to about 15.2m (50 feet) long could use the centre line only, but longer narrowboats may need a bow line in addition to prevent the bow swinging across the chamber.
- Progressively open the ground paddle on the same side of the chamber as the boat. The flow of water will hold the boat alongside until the lock is about half full. Now you can cross the lock and open the other ground paddle.
- If the lock has gate paddles as well then once the paddle holes are submerged you can open these progressively.

- Use the lines or your engine, to keep the bow clear of the top gate and to avoid drifting backwards and catching the stern on the bottom gates.
- To conserve water share the lock with another boat (or boats). If a steel narrowboat is sharing with a GRP boat, the narrowboat enters the lock first, and the GRP exits first.
- Use lines to hold the boats steady against the lock sides. Again a centre line or 'lazy line' works well in canal locks.
- Ensure that the bows of both boats are level and open the top ground paddles together, equally and progressively, followed by the gate paddles.
- When full, open the gates, motor out, and then close the gates and paddles behind you.

Problems - going up

Make sure that your boat doesn't get caught on the gates. If it does, close the top paddles immediately. Now open a bottom paddle to lower the water level and free the boat. Do not tie or pass ropes around lock ladders or anything else inside the lock chamber. They will disappear underwater as the lock fills.

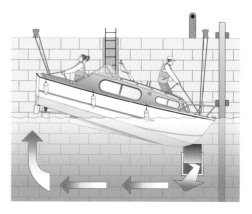

Going downhill

- When approaching the lock, drop a crew member off to go ahead and prepare the lock.

- If the lock is empty, check for approaching craft coming uphill and let them use the lock first – it conserves water and is good manners.

- If the lock is free and empty, make sure that the bottom gates and paddles are closed as (a) in fig 1.

- Fill the lock by opening the top paddles (b).

- Open the top gates and close top paddles.

- Enter the lock and close the top gates.

- Progressively open one, then the other, bottom paddle (a).

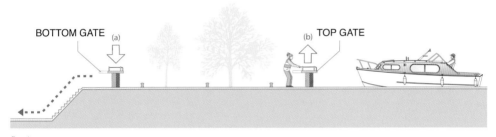

fig 1

- As you descend, hold the boat steady with lines passed round bollards. Do not tie them off. Make sure they 'pay out' smoothly.

- Use your engine to keep the boat in position if necessary.

- Make sure that the boat's gunwales and guards do not catch on the lock edges as the boat goes down.

- Keep the bows away from the bottom gates and the stern clear of the cill behind.

- When the lock is empty, open the bottom gates and exit.

- Close the bottom paddles (a).

- Close the gates (unless another boat is approaching).

fig 2

Problems - going downhill

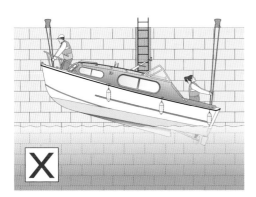

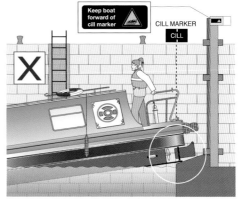

This is what can happen if you tie up in a lock

Do not cut the lines. Close the bottom paddles and refill lock to refloat the boat.

To avoid the cill, keep your boat's stern and rudder at least six feet away from the top gate.

On longer narrowboats (60ft plus) keep the bow as close to the bottom gate as possible (within 12") without actually touching the gate.

If your boat does get caught on the cill, close the bottom paddles immediately.

Open one top paddle gently. The boat will then float off.

Do not turn the prop until you are absolutely sure that there is no damage to the rudder, skeg or prop.

In recent years the Canal & River Trust have introduced 'cill markers' to all locks. This is a white line on a black background painted on the edge of the lock side by the top gates to show the extent to which the lock cill protrudes into the chamber below. There is also a yellow warning sign fixed to the gate beam next to it with the words "Keep boat forward of cill marker".

When the lock is full, water covers the cill so you cannot see it. If you position your boat too near the top gate, as the water level falls the stern will become caught on the cill, causing severe damage, injury and even sinking.

Keep boat forward of cill marker

Conserving water

Each time a boat goes through a lock, up to 50,000 gallons of water are used. Canal reservoirs depend on rain to replenish supplies but in the summer, levels can get very low.

So follow the **THRIFT** Code:

Two in a lock. Share a lock whenever you can with another boat.

Have you shut all paddles and gates behind you?

Report any leaks or damage to the local navigation staff.

Invite any oncoming boats through if the lock is set against you.

Follow advice and instructions given by navigation staff.

Timings can change. Check for any lock restrictions and closures.

River locks on larger navigations

On commercial navigations and principal rivers such as the Thames and Severn, the locks are much larger than conventional ones. They are mostly keeper-operated and may have traffic lights (see page 78).

Most are mechanised and some have limited opening hours (check the relevant guide book).

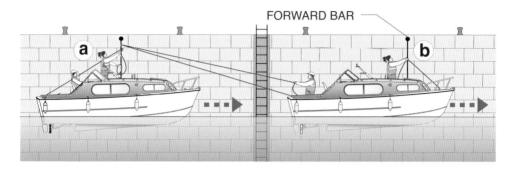

In the lock, bring the stern line forward (**a**) and pass around the bar or bollard in the lock wall, then motor forward, paying out the line (**b**). Pass the bow line round the forward bar or bollard, and centre your boat between the two points.

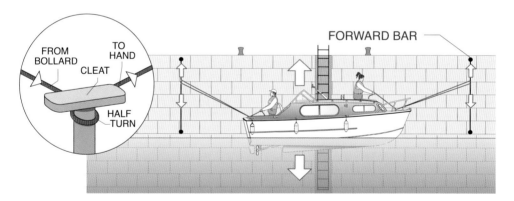

Do not tie the lines off. Take a half turn around your boat cleat and hold the line, adjusting as necessary.

Beware of the turbulence created as the paddles are raised. Keep the lines taut to prevent surging and adjust as necessary as you rise.

Going down is less turbulent. Pay out the lines as you descend making sure they do not jam.

Staircase locks - going uphill

Two, three, four, or even five locks joined together are called a staircase.
The top gates of one lock are also the bottom gates of the next one.

There are two main types of staircase:
1. The water from the lock above flows into a side pond which then fills the lock below.
2. As illustrated, the water from each lock goes directly into the lock below. Most staircases are controlled by lock keepers. Always follow their directions. The rule is, only open one lock at a time.

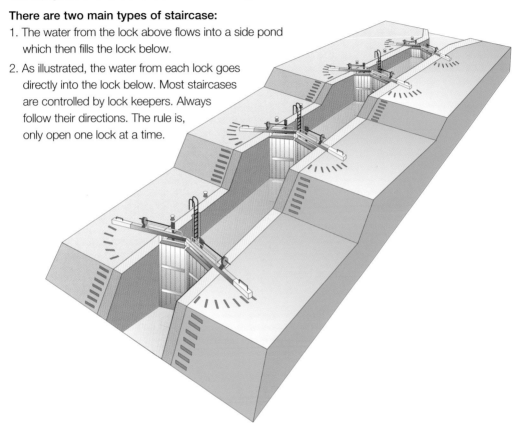

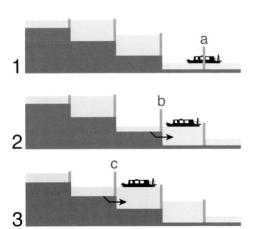

Going uphill
Prepare all the locks in a staircase before you enter the first lock. The bottom one should be empty, the rest full.

1. Enter the bottom lock and close the bottom gates and paddles (**a**).
2. Open the paddles (**b**) to fill the bottom lock from the middle lock.
   When the bottom lock is full, move into the middle lock. Close the gates and paddles behind you.
3. Open the paddles (**c**) of the next lock and repeat the process as before.

Going downhill

Prepare all the locks in the staircase before you enter the first lock. The top one should be full, the rest empty.

1. Enter the top lock and close the top gates and paddles behind you (**a**).
2. Open the bottom paddles (**b**). The water from the top lock will fill the middle lock.
3. When the top and middle lock levels are equal, move into the middle lock (**c**). Close the gates and paddles behind you and repeat the process as before.

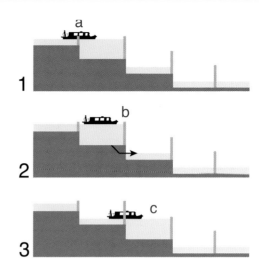

Problems - going downhill

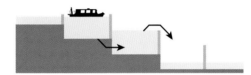

Make sure that the lower lock is empty enough to take all the water from above. If not, it will overflow.

Always check that every gate and paddle behind you is closed before opening the paddles in front of you. If not, the lock above may completely drain. Also make sure that the paddles beyond the ones you are working on are closed otherwise the water will continue out through the next lock.

Problems - going uphill

Make sure that the upper lock is full enough to fill the lock below. If not, you will run out of water. Check that every gate and paddle behind you is closed before opening the paddles in front of you. Otherwise you will lose all your water. After you have finished setting all the locks at the beginning, make sure that all paddles are closed.

- When working through a staircase always make sure that 'everything behind you is closed before opening anything in front of you!'
- Nearly all staircase locks are controlled by lock keepers in the season so moor up and go to find the keeper first. They will advise you when it's your turn to start through the flight and offer advice should you need it.

Guillotine locks

You will find lots of these locks on the River Nene and Great Ouse systems.

To empty the lock, once the top gates and paddles are closed, raise the bottom gate by winding it up a few turns only. Once empty, raise the gate fully and exit.
Some guillotine locks have power operation.

On some unmanned river locks you may have to leave the lock empty with the downstream sluices slightly open (look in the appropriate guide book).

On the River Nene, for instance, you also have to leave the downstream "guillotine" gate open (up). If you are heading upstream and there is a boat waiting to come downstream into the lock then obviously don't empty it. However, if no boat is waiting, still have a good look upstream for an approaching boat before you empty the lock, as they will really appreciate you leaving it ready for them, and it saves you some work as well.

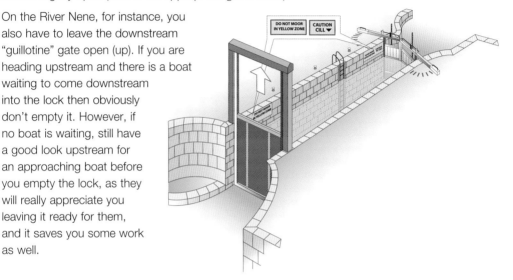

Twin locks

These can be either narrow or broad.
You can use either lock but where possible use the one set in your favour.

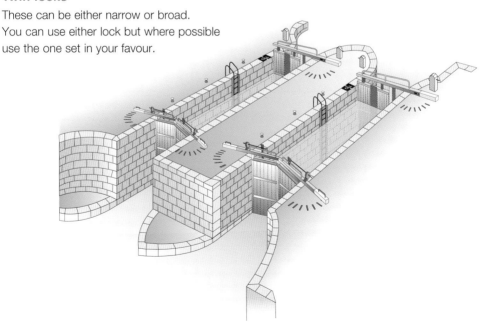

Canal bridges

Admiring the architecture of canal bridges is one of the delights of any cruise. They all have their individual styles which vary from canal to canal. However, all the bridges on an individual canal will have a common width and minimum headroom. Check the relevant guide book for this important information! The conventional canal bridge is usually a 'hump-back' design made from brick or stone. Most modern replacements have flat decks. All have bridge numbers or names.

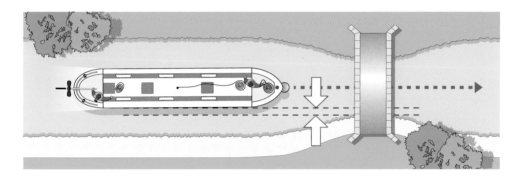

Navigating canal bridges
- Warn the crew to beware of low bridges and keep within the profile of the boat.
- The channel narrows at bridges and the arch is usually lower on the non-towpath side.
- Take down vulnerable chimneys, aerials, etc.
- Check for any boats coming the other way. If the other boat is nearer, give way. Slow down early, keep to the right and wave them on.
- Resume your course when they have passed. If you have to stop, don't reverse too hard, or your boat may turn sideways (broach) and block the channel.
- Line the boat up early and look along the side of the boat. Aim to miss the towpath through the bridge by 6-12 inches.
- Slow down as you go through otherwise your prop may pick up sunken rubbish under the bridge. You may even need to go through in neutral if it's bad.

River bridges

River bridge architecture is often ancient, with many structures dating from before the Norman conquest of 1066 and others not much younger! They more often than not have several arches, sometimes seven or more. Their arches are usually pointed at the top which gives reduced air draught (headroom) at the sides.

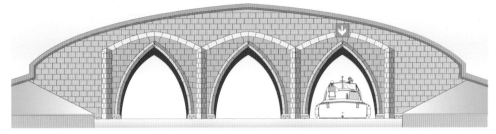

Navigating river bridges

- First, ascertain which arch to use. The navigation span in your direction will not usually be the same as in the other. It should be marked above the arch, often with a blue board and a white arrow pointing down.
- If a boat is coming the other way and is heading downstream, they have priority. You should slow right down against the current to let them through.
- Motor through the bridge using the same techniques as with canal bridges, but stay in the middle of the arch (where the headroom is greatest - there are no towpaths through river bridges).

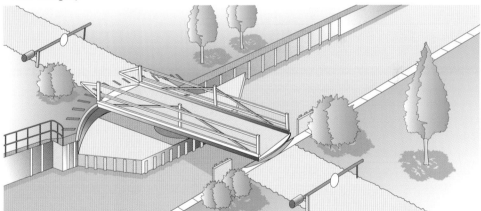

Manual swing bridges

- To operate these your crew will have to cross the bridge to the non-towpath side.
- Set your crew off at the landing stage with windlass and C&RT key. If it is a heavy manual bridge, you may need more than one crew.
- If it is a traffic bridge, check that the road is clear. Many have traffic barriers which must be closed before the bridge is opened.

- Unhook the retaining chain or hasp and steadily push the bridge open.
- Slow the bridge down as it reaches the end of the swing so that it doesn't bounce back across the canal.
- Once the boat is through, shut the bridge and secure it with the chain or hasp.
- Don't forget to re-open the traffic safety barriers before you get back on board.
- On powered swing bridges use the Watermate key and operate the mechanism.

Lifting bridge

- To operate these your crew will have to cross the bridge to the non-towpath side.
- Set your crew off at the landing stage with windlass and C&RT key. If it is a heavy bridge, you may need more than one crew.
- If it is a traffic bridge, check that the road is clear and close the barriers.
- Pull the chain down and sit on the beam to hold the bridge open. This is very important - bridges have been known to fall on boats.
- On winch drum or hydraulic bridges, make sure that any latches or catches are in place.
- When the boat is through, gently lower the bridge. Do not let it drop.
- Re-open the traffic barriers and re-board the boat.

Mechanised swing or lifting bridge

These bridges vary greatly in size and operation. On larger waterways they are operated by keepers and have traffic lights (see page 78).

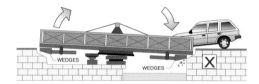

- Come alongside at the landing stage and set your crew down (with windlass and C&RT key). Brief the crew to read and understand the operating instructions on the control panel BEFORE they lower the traffic barriers!
- Lower the traffic barriers, then, on powered bridges, insert the key and start the opening sequence. On manual bridges, unlock the wedges and then use the windlass to wind the bridge open.
- When the boat is through, start the closing sequence or wind close, then raise the traffic barriers.

Most mechanised bridges have wedges so that they don't bounce when vehicles cross them. Please ensure that these are firmly back in place before you leave. Otherwise vehicles could damage the mechanism.

Movable bridge safety tips
- Make sure that you push (or pole or use the bowthruster) to ensure that the boat moves out into the centre of the channel so you pass through the bridge squarely.
- Make sure that there is nobody on the roof, foredeck or in the well deck as you pass through.

- Watch out for crosswinds.
- Don't let the boat arrive too early – if the bridge is not properly open there will be no time to stop before a dangerous collision.

Never allow children or passers-by to operate the bridge for you.

Safety tips

- On approaching the tunnel, switch on the tunnel light and get your crew to switch on all the interior lights, opening the curtains so that light shines on the tunnel walls.
- Have a lantern or large torch on the cabin roof at the stern to shine onto the right-hand tunnel wall.
- Brief all crew to keep within the profile of the boat. Youngsters in the well deck must be supervised!
- Sound your horn as you approach.
- Wear a light waterproof. Most tunnels drip!
- Height gauges are placed at each end of low tunnels. If your boat's cabin hits the gauge, do not proceed – you could get wedged halfway through!
- Tunnels vary in length and width: generally on broad canals two narrowboats can pass, and the same is true on some

narrow waterways. On other narrow canals however, there is only room for one. Check the relevant guide book and at the tunnel entrance for any special instructions. So if it's a narrow tunnel and a boat is in it coming your way you must wait.

- Some tunnels have traffic lights to show when you can go through.
- One tunnel even has tunnel keepers to control the traffic.

Navigating tunnels

- Upon entering remove sunglasses and try to get your eyes used to the dark quickly, whilst keeping your speed down and staying in the centre.
- Do not move the tiller too much.

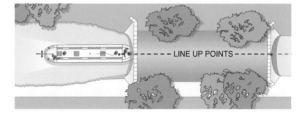

LINE UP POINTS

- Most tunnels have several air shafts. Try to avoid the temptation to look up at them as you pass underneath. Otherwise you will get a face full of cold water and lose your 'night sight'!

It's common to feel that you are going to one side. Keep a point on the cabin top in line with the pin point of light at the other end. Don't over-compensate or you will zig-zag badly. In wide tunnels, look out for approaching craft. Slow right down and pass on the right. Keep your light on until you've come out at the other end, to warn approaching boats.

Emergencies: Do not stop unless you break down. If you have to stop:

- Turn the engine off to avoid fumes building up.
- Sound long horn blasts to attract attention.
- If you can't cure the problem, push the boat out using the boat pole. All tunnels have a continuous wooden baulk running along one side just above the waterline

with loops of chain hung from it. These can be used to help poling. Alternatively, walk it along the tunnel walls. ("Legging" just like the old boatmen used to do.)

- There are luminous arrows in the tunnel roof indicating the shortest route out. Also there are signs on the walls showing the shortest route with the distance in metres.
- Do not swim out.
- Mobile phones do not work in tunnels.

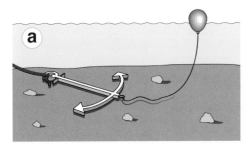

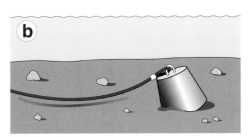

If you think the anchor may get stuck, add a tripping line (**a**) to the other end of the anchor so you can pull it free.

A mud weight (**b**) is often used as a non-snagging anchor when there's little or no current.

Any Inland waterway boat using a river must carry an approved anchor, chain and line. This is a requirement of the Boat Safety Scheme. It is carried as the 'emergency brake' if your engine fails or your propeller becomes fouled.

On a narrow fast flowing waterway, keep the anchor at the upstream end of the boat to act as a brake in an emergency.

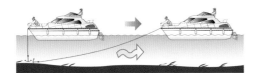

Dropping the anchor

Have the anchor rope ready (about six times the depth of water) to pay out as soon as the boat stops.

Drop the anchor and reverse back slowly paying out the line.

When the correct amount is out, make fast and apply a little extra power astern to help the anchor dig in.

Getting the anchor up (weighing anchor)

Often, the crew can just pull the line in, but in a strong wind or current, a touch of ahead will take the load off as the crew pulls in the slack.

If the anchor is stuck, make the anchor line fast when the rope is upright and let the momentum of the boat break it out of the bottom.

- Hire boats are not allowed to navigate after dark.
- Cruising in the dark can be dangerous and the inexperienced are advised not to.
- On rivers, all boats must have navigation lights.
- On canals, a narrowboat must have at least a white light showing to the front.
- Take extra care if using locks at night. Accidents are far more likely and it is easy to inadvertently leave a paddle up and waste water.

Note that a tunnel light is not the same as a navigation light.

Navigation Lights

A WHITE light front and back

A **GREEN** light on the right (starboard) side

A **RED** light on the left (port) side

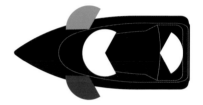

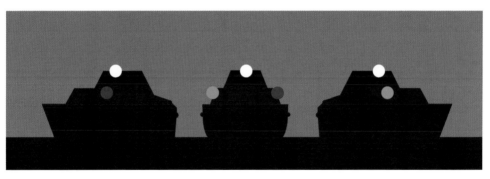

These navigation lights can tell you which way another boat is going:

White above red – crossing from right to left.
White above green and red – coming towards you.
White above green – crossing from left to right.

Note: Small boats may show a single all round white light or a combined red/green bow light.

These are the usual sound signals. Check your local waterways book for more information. Be prepared, others might not know their meaning.

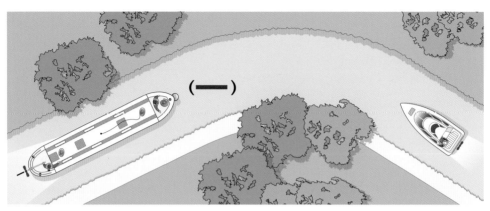

Sound a long blast every 20 seconds when approaching a blind bend or bridge. Position a crew member forward as a look-out.

MAKE SURE THAT OTHERS KNOW YOUR INTENTIONS:

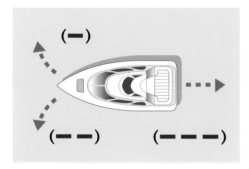

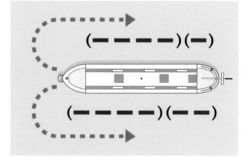

(—)

One short blast
I AM TURNING TO THE RIGHT (STARBOARD)

(— —)

Two short blasts
I AM TURNING TO THE LEFT (PORT)

(— — —)

Three short blasts
OPERATING ASTERN PROPULSION
(NOT NECESSARILY GOING ASTERN))

(——)

One extra long blast
WARNING AT TUNNELS, BLIND BENDS AND
JUNCTIONS

(— — — —)(—)

Four short blasts, pause, then one short blast
I AM TURNING AROUND TO MY RIGHT
(STARBOARD)

(— — — —)(— —)

Four short blasts, pause, then two short blasts
I AM TURNING AROUND TO MY LEFT (PORT)

(— — — — —)

Five or more short blasts
YOUR INTENTIONS ARE UNCLEAR or ARE
YOU TAKING SUFFICIENT AVOIDING ACTION?

On some British rivers and canals, lock keepers can be contacted by VHF radio. This is more common abroad.

If using VHF, at least one person on board must hold a valid operator's certificate, such as the SRC. It is also a requirement for every boat fitted with a VHF radiotelephone to be covered by a Ship Radio Licence.

Registration for and renewals of Ship Radio Licences are free.

Recent legislative changes by the Port of London Authority on the tidal River Thames make it necessary for the operator of any boat over 45 feet in length to carry a VHF radio.

EUROPEAN REQUIREMENTS

In other European countries, there are a number of requirements for vessels using inland waterways.

For example you may be required to carry a copy of the Inland Waterway Rules (CEVNI).

All British vessels also have to be registered if cruising outside British waters and an International Certificate of Competence (ICC) may be necessary, depending on the country you are visiting. The ICC must be endorsed for inland waterways use.

Ship radio licences are issued by:
OFCOM, Licensing Centre,
PO Box 56373, London, SE1 9SZ
Tel: 020 7981 3131
Web: www.ofcom.org.uk/licensing/olc

For more information on any of the above, contact the RYA on 02380 604 100 or visit their website: www.rya.org.uk

When going upstream, **red** buoys or cylindrical markers define the port (left) side of the channel.
Posts can be all red, or have white bands.
A flashing red light may show at night.

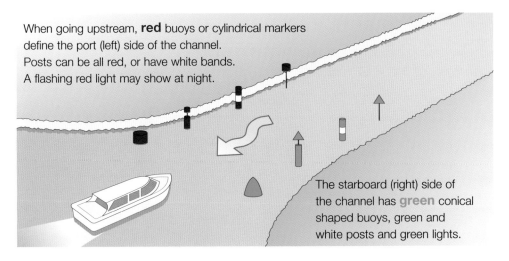

The starboard (right) side of the channel has green conical shaped buoys, green and white posts and green lights.

BUOYS AND LIGHTS ARE THE OTHER WAY ROUND WHEN GOING DOWNSTREAM

TRAFFIC LIGHTS

When used at locks and bridges traffic lights have similar meanings to those used on highways and must be obeyed.

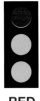

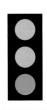

RED
STOP
do not pass
this light

RED and
GREEN
GET READY
TO PROCEED
but do not
pass the red light

GREEN
GO

AMBER
PROCEED
WITH CAUTION

DREDGING OR WORKS

Pass the dredger on the side showing the white or green lights or diamond shapes. Do not pass on the side showing red lights or ball shapes. But, beware: on canals, the edges of works or restrictions on both sides are often marked with red lights or red squares by day irrespective of whether you are going upstream or downstream.

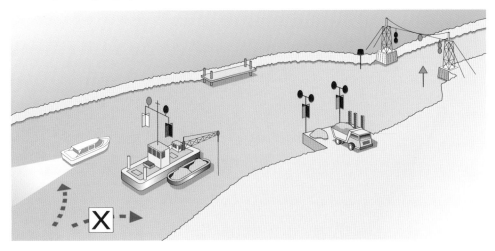

WARNING SIGNS

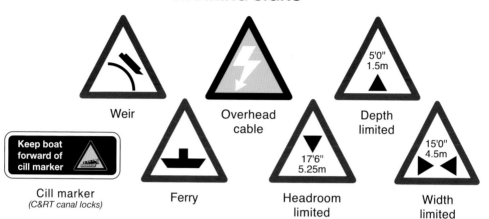

Weir

Overhead cable

5'0"
1.5m

Depth limited

Keep boat forward of cill marker

Cill marker
(C&RT canal locks)

Ferry

17'6"
5.25m

Headroom limited

15'0"
4.5m

Width limited

PROHIBITORY SIGNS

No entry

No

No overtaking

No anchoring

No mooring

No pump out

No refuse disposal

No turning

Do not create wash

No fishing

No motor boats

No swimming

No shooting

MANDATORY SIGNS

Beware

Use this
radio channel

Sound horn

Speed limit

Move over or turn in this direction

One-way

Cross channel
to left

Cross channel
to right

Keep to the side of the
channel on your left side

Keep to the side of the
channel on your right side

INFORMATIVE SIGNS

Water (cold)

Refuse
disposal

Chemical closet
disposal unit

Mooring
often with time limit

Telephone

Toilets

Winding point

Tunnel

Disabled

Water tap

Toilet pump
out

Showers

Turning place

Lifting bridge

Lock

Serviced lock *(R. Thames locks)*

Self service *(R. Thames locks)*

Different navigation authorities may use different regulations. Make sure you have a copy of the relevant reference books on board. In mainland Europe most countries use a common system based on CEVNI.

Bank effect	Interaction between prop and water drawing boat towards bank
Bilges	Space in hull beneath deck of boat
Bollard	Fitting on bank for attaching mooring lines
Bottom effect	Interaction between boat and shallow bottom of waterway
Bowthruster	Small prop mounted sideways in bow to assist manoeuvring
Centre line	Handling line attached to fixing point at centre of narrowboat
CEVNI	European Inland Waterway Rules
Cill	Protruding part of lock structure below top gates
Cleat	Deck fitting to which mooring lines are attached
Cut	Alternative name for canal
Fender	Cushions impact by boat with bank, jetty or another boat
Grab rail	Hand rail
Guillotine locks	Locks with gates which are raised vertically
Gunwale	Top edge of hull
Helm	Steering the boat – steering position
Interaction	Interaction between prop and water drawing boat towards bank or another boat
'Lazy line'	Handling line attached to fixing point at centre of cruiser
'Legging'	Manual method of propelling boat through tunnel
Lock	Means of moving boat to new level of water
MOB	Man overboard
Outdrive	Steerable drive from inboard engine through hull
Paddle gear	Shutters for controlling water filling or emptying locks
'Paddle wheel' effect	Sideways movement of boat which occurs when prop is used
Piling hook	Device for attaching mooring line to piling
Pivot point	Theoretical point around which boat pivots
Pound	Stretch of water between locks on canals
'Prop effect/walk'	Sideways movement of boat which occurs when prop is used
Pulpit	Guard rail around bow of boat
Pump-out station	Place where toilet holding tanks and bilges can be emptied
Push pit	Guard rail around stern of boat
Reach	Stretch of water between locks on rivers
Reverse bank effect	Interaction between prop and water pushing boat away from bank
Riser board	Vertical rubbing board protecting lock gate and boat from damage
Sanitary station	Service station for emptying portable toilets
Sluice	Device for controlling flow of water (*see also* Paddle gear)
Spring lines	Mooring lines from bow or stern towards centre of bank/jetty
Springing off	Method of leaving mooring using spring line
Staircase locks	Series of locks where the bottom gates of the one above are also the top gates of the one below
Stern drive	Steerable drive from inboard engine through hull
Stern tube	Tube with bearing through which prop shaft passes out of boat
Swaging	Tightening mooring line
Swigging	Tightening mooring line
Tee stud	Deck fitting to which mooring lines are attached
Tiller	Steering handle attached to rudder
Towpath	Path beside canal, used originally for horses towing boats
'Transverse thrust'	Sideways movement of boat which occurs when prop is used
'Watermate' key	Key issued by the Canal & River Trust to unlock paddle gear etc
Weed hatch	Access hatch for clearing prop on narrowboat
Weil's Disease	Disease spread by rats in water
Well deck	Deck at bow of narrowboat
Winding hole	Boat turning place
Windlass	Handle for operating lock paddles

The following pages describe the syllabus for the RYA Inland Waterways Helmsman's course. Due to time constraints and variations in course locations and equipment, not all subjects can be covered in great detail or practically when afloat. We have therefore specified three levels of teaching to show you in how much depth you can expect each item to be covered.

These three levels are:

KNOWLEDGE OF: The subject will be briefly explained. Familiarisation occurs during the course and information on where to find out more is given.

UNDERSTANDS: The subject will be covered in more depth. You will be asked to demonstrate a basic understanding and go away from the course able to develop further your own skill in this area. Confirmation of your understanding of the subject may be achieved in a number of ways, such as question and answer sessions.

CAN: The subject will be covered in greater depth, including background theory, practical coaching and repeated practice by yourself until you can demonstrate the required level of skill in this subject.

INLAND WATERWAYS CREW COURSE

For friends or family members to have a better understanding of how they can assist the helm.

Minimum age: Eight

Duration: One day

Instructor to student ratio: 1:3

Personal Safety

Understands:

- The difference between life jackets and buoyancy aids

- Appropriate clothing

- Moving around the boat safely

Can:

- Correctly fit a life jacket or buoyancy aid

Signature of instructor

Deckwork

Understands:

- Preparation of mooring lines
- Communication and the importance of letting the helm know when they have slipped or attached the lines
- Common nautical terms

Can:

- Attach fenders (if used)
- Coil a line
- Throw a mooring line
- Attach a line to a cleat, dolly or t-stud

Signature of instructor

Boat Handling

Understands:

- The importance of crew communication

Can:

- Start and stop the engine
- Steer and control boat speed

Signature of instructor

Locks

Knowledge of:

- How locks work

Can:

- Tend lines in a lock
- Operate or assist in the operation of gates and paddles

Signature of instructor

Collision Avoidance

Knowledge of:

- Basic rules of the waterway

Can:

- Keep a lookout

Signature of instructor

Emergency Situations

Knowledge of:

- Problems that can happen on the inland waterways
- Preventing fire

Understands:

- Their role in an emergency
- How to raise the alarm
- How to prevent MOB
- The MOB recovery procedure for their vessel

Can:

- Stop the boat
- Locate first aid kit
- Use a boathook

Signature of instructor

Environment

Knowledge of:

- Potential impact of boating on the environment and how to minimise this
- Recycling
- How to read a waterways map

Signature of instructor

INLAND WATERWAYS HELMSMAN'S COURSE

To give students the confidence to helm a vessel safely on the Inland Waterways

Minimum age: 12

Duration: Two days

Instructor to student ratio: 1:3

Endorsement (tick if it applies):

Is aged 12–16 and therefore the holder should only use powered craft under the supervision of a responsible adult	☐
Assistance required to complete the course	☐

Personal Safety

Understands:

- The risks involved with ending up in the water, including cold shock
- Avoidance of personal injury, including crush injuries when fending off
- Special risks to children

Can:

- Correctly fit a buoyancy aid or life jacket

Signature of instructor

Engines

Understands:

- Checks to be undertaken periodically

Can:

- Undertake checks to be carried out before and whilst running

Signature of instructor

Deckwork

Knowledge of:

- Common boating terms

Can:

- Handling warps and fenders (if used)
- Throwing a heaving line or coiled rope
- Tie the following:
    - Clove hitch
    - Round turn and two half-hitches
    - Bowline
- Secure to:
    - Bollards
    - Rings
    - Cleats
    - Mooring stakes

Signature of instructor

Helmsmanship and Boat Handling

Knowledge of:

- Berthing and unberthing between piles

Understands:

- Loading and weight distribution
- Inter-action and canal effect
- Anchoring
- Pivot points

Can:

- Carefully steer a vessel
- Turn a vessel around
- Berth alongside
- Recover a man overboard dummy

Signature of instructor

Locks

Understands:

- Maintenance of levels

Can:

- Operate a lock
- Tend lines in a lock

Signature of instructor

Bridges and Tunnels

Understands:

- Bridge operations
- Use of tunnels

Signature of instructor

Collision Avoidance

Knowledge of:

- The Rules of the Road

Understands:

- By-laws and local traffic regulations
- National regulations
- Publications to be carried

Signature of instructor

Boat Safety

Knowledge of:

- Use of fire extinguishers
- Watertight integrity

Understands:

- Fire hazards, particularly gas and petrol
- Refloating after grounding
- The risks of CO poisoning

Signature of instructor

Care of the Environment

Understands:

- Avoiding damage to banks, boats, flora and fauna
- Pollution avoidance
- Consideration for water users

Signature of instructor

Direct Assessment for Experienced Helms

The candidate should have the equivalent of at least one full season's helming on the inland waterways.

Practical assessment: the candidate should be able to demonstrate, without tuition, all of the practical elements of the Inland Waterways Helmsman's Course syllabus (the 'Can' aspects).

Theory assessment: the candidate should be able to answer satisfactorily questions on the theoretical elements of the Inland Waterways Helmsman's Course syllabus (the 'Knowledge of' and 'Understands' aspects).

If you enjoyed this book, you may be interested in:

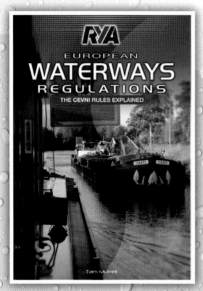

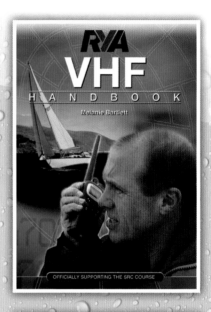

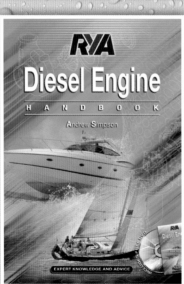

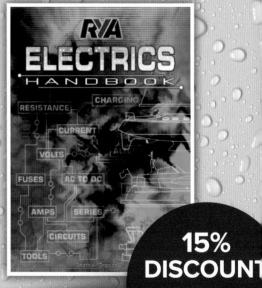

eBooks

Many of our eBooks include animations, videos and interactive tools to enhance learning.

There are multiple ways to buy eBooks.

Download the RYA Books App

Buy via Apple Books and Google Play

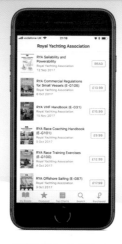

Find out more:
**www.rya.org.uk/
go/ebooks**

WHY JOIN THE RYA?

OVER 80

RYA member
reward partners

Influencing policy on over
250 marine protected
areas in UK waters

Fighting for members'
rights on more than
20 Current Affairs topics

OnBoard has
introduced over

800,000

children to sailing

60,000+

disabled people have
been able to experience
sailing through the RYA
Sailability programme

Membership costs
from only

12p per day

2,500 international training
centres including the UK,
Australia, New Zealand,
South Africa, Indonesia,
Thailand and the USA

250,000

course completions
each year

OVER
815,000

visits to our Knowledge
and Advice web
pages a year